GROWING UP:
AN AMERICAN BOYHOOD,
1945-1965

S T E P H E N   M A C D O N A L D

To order additional copies of this book, contact:
Xlibris
844-714-8691
www.Xlibris.com
Orders@Xlibris.com

ISBN: Softcover   978-1-6641-6680-6
        Hardcover   978-1-6641-6681-3
        EBook   978-1-6641-6679-0

Print information available on the last page

Rev. date: 04/14/2021

To my sisters: Ann, Brenda, Mary, and Patty

And to my wife Mary Warner and my son John MacDonald

Really, one might almost live one's life over, if only one could make sufficient effort of recollection.

John Banville

ACKNOWLEDGEMENTS

A number of people assisted me in writing this memoir.

Above all, I am deeply grateful to my wife, Mary Warner, whose enthusiasm for the project buoyed and encouraged me from the outset. Mary is a splendid writer, a sensitive reader and a fastidious, indefatigable editor. She read the entire manuscript closely twice and made countless astute suggestions that helped me to tighten, clarify and improve the language. I could not have written the memoir without her.

In seeking to settle details of family history, I asked my sisters--Ann McGuiggin, Mary Modoono, and Patty Otis--to respond to a series of questions that I posed. The answers these good women provided me were very helpful as I assembled the narrative. I hope they are pleased with what I have written here.

Several old friends who appear in these pages read all or part of the text as it emerged and their favorable assessment of what I was doing encouraged me to persist. My thanks to Tom McKelvey, Alex Humez, Jean McMahon Humez and Steve Johnson. Thanks, as well, to Eric Handley, for tracking down some of his old photographs from high school.

Stephen MacDonald
Harrisburg, Pa.
January, 2021

FORWARD

This is what I remember about growing up between 1945 and 1965 in the United States.

Those 20 years in American history may have been the easiest years--comfortable, prosperous, secure years--to grow up if you were white and male and middle class and didn't get polio. It was the moment when the United States had just triumphed in the most destructive war in history and emerged as the greatest military, political and economic force on the planet. The country was poised to embark on an exuberant financial and cultural expansion that would bring many of its people unprecedented prosperity.

My family did not participate in that prosperity. Our economic fortunes declined and the extended family fell apart. We abruptly separated from my grandmother and aunts. My father's professional and personal life collapsed; he lost his job, and my parents divorced. My mother held her brood together, barely. We survived. There was, in the end, no tragedy; this is not a sad story. I had what I actually sometimes imagined to be a happy childhood, though the truth was that I grew up in a fraught and fragile place riven by domestic disarray and scandal.

This is a memoir, not a family history, but I talk a lot about my family in these pages. While I proceed more or less chronologically, I abandon the conventions of chronology when it seems more interesting to address things topically. I have not consulted documents in any systematic way. I've asked questions of my sisters, and they have helped me sort out narrative details and prodded my recollections. But the story here is personal; my sisters have their own stories to tell.

What happens in these 20 years unfolds, for the most part, in a confined space--almost all of it in Massachusetts. It took place within a radius of just nine miles slightly north and west of Boston. I lived from 1945 to 1950 in the city of Malden, from 1950 to 1955 in the town of Burlington, from 1955 to 1965 in the town of Lexington. The only violation of this intimate geography occurred in the decade's final two years--from 1963 to 1965--when I was carried off to the other side of the world in the United States Army. We'll get to that....

MY FAMILY

I was born in March 1945, in Malden, Massachusetts--seven weeks before the end of the European war that would come to absorb so much of my imagination. My mother, Marguerite MacDonald, was 30 years old. She had been working, until shortly before my birth, as a civilian draftsperson for the Army Signal Corps, the kind of wartime employment that women took on in those years as men were sucked away into the Army. My father, Charles MacDonald, was 32 years old and worked in nearby Somerville as office manager for the Jerguson Gage and Valve Company which manufactured specialized control systems for submarines. This defense–related work and the fact that he already had two other children--my eight-year-old sister Ann and six-year-old sister Brenda--shielded him from the draft.

My mother and I on the left and her friend, Dot Morganti,
and her son, on the right. Malden. April 1945.

Malden was a densely-packed, working-class place of about 60,000 people five miles from downtown Boston. My parents had always lived there. But our families were relative newcomers to the United States.

My father's grandfather--my great-great-grandfather--had been born in Scotland, I'm told, and had immigrated, first to Canada--to Nova Scotia, actually--and then eventually to Boston. My father's father, Albert MacDonald, was born in Boston, making my father just a second generation American. My father's mother, Catherine McNeil, was American by birth. She was very beautiful, they say, with long auburn hair. She died young, in her late 30s, of tuberculosis, and grandfather Albert never remarried.

My mother's people, on both sides, had only recently come to America. My great grandmother had been born in County Cork in Ireland, on the southwestern coast. I don't know when she immigrated to the United States. My maternal grandfather, the formidable John Perry, was an Englishman, born in Liverpool. My mother maintained that John Perry's father had been a captain in the Royal Navy and that the young John had left England as a teenager to seek his fortune in the New World in the first decade of the 20th century. I'm dubious about that story. Would an officer of the line of the Royal Navy permit his son to head off to America for uncertain adventures? Anyway, young John landed in Boston, became a postal clerk in the U.S Postal Service, and fell in love with the beautiful Irish-American, Margaret Lucey. She was Catholic, of course, and he was Protestant, of course. He converted. There's one story that her parents were so scandalized that she was marrying a Protestant--and an Englishman--that they did not attend the wedding. There's another story that her parents were delighted and issued handsome wedding invitations and gave the couple a lovely brass clock as a gift.

I never knew my grandfather John: he died of a massive stroke when I was six months old in the fall of 1945. My grandparents had five children: three daughters--Marguerite, May, and Katherine--and two sons, Francis and John, the latter of whom died as an infant.

Marguerite was called Peggy or Peg. She was intelligent and possessed a charismatic dark beauty; she was quick and vivacious and ambitious. She was her father's favorite. Her younger sister May had a soft blond loveliness and projected an attractive calm. Another sister, Katherine--Kay--was small and nervous and always aflutter. Everyone called their brother Francis, Frank. He was short and vulpine.

MY PARENTS

I don't think I ever really knew my father. Charlie MacDonald was a handsome man and had a strong physical presence, but I don't remember seeing much of him or our doing much together. We hardly ever played or wrestled or roughhoused. A couple of times he tickled me and rubbed his beard on my belly and got me in a hammerlock. Great fun, but infrequent. He was remote; he usually called me "son." We never, I think, played catch and so I didn't really learn how to throw a baseball. He took me to my Little League games but he didn't stay to watch me play. When the marriage to my mother broke up and he left, I didn't miss him. It's ungrateful to say that.

Charles MacDonald, Stephen MacDonald, Albert MacDonald.

My mother was the center of the family. Peg MacDonald was electric and bright and lots of fun to be with. She was beautiful and unsentimental and made of dark steel. She laughed easily and played the piano. She was a shrewd judge of character; she did not like stupid people and she could be preemptory and ferocious. She loved her children and was their strongest advocate. She also assessed them carefully. She had high standards for behavior and comportment. She did not appreciate people, even children, who whined or cried or failed to speak clearly or who did not demonstrate resilience in the face of setbacks. She liked people who were strong. You did not go to her to be cuddled.

My mother.

As the only boy in a brood of girls, I was a favorite of my mother. I was also, thank God, like Ann, a "Perry," blessed with my mother's dark eyes and hair, unlike the "MacDonalds," my poor blond sisters Brenda and Mary and Patty. As the boy, I was often excused from "girls' work" like housecleaning or doing the dishes that my mother would assign to my sisters so that "Stevie can read." This was an enormous advantage of which I made outrageous use. I was to be spared demeaning feminizing tasks that might interfere with the successful arc of my boyhood. My mother, of course, wanted this one son of hers to be a success, to be "a real boy."

But I'm not sure she was ever quite sure who I was or what "a real boy" was supposed to be like. How could she be? Surrounded by all those girls, and lacking a consistent paternal guide or model, I wasn't altogether certain what "a real boy" was supposed to be either. I was quiet and bookish; I liked to read; I liked to draw pictures. Is this what real boys were supposed to be? I think both my mother and I may have distrusted my preternatural talent as an artist. It somehow came too easily. This clearly reminded my mother of her own gifts. Who knows where it came from, but I could do it! She liked the fact that I could do it and was proud of me, but she worried, I believe, that I might be tempted to pursue a career in the field of art, and she felt that that would be a mistake, not only because such careers are often poorly paid but, even more so, because a man working in the art world may be, in some people's eyes, insufficiently masculine, may be regarded as effeminate and not be "a real man."

96 BELMONT ST.

When I was born my family lived on Oliver Street in a neighborhood in Malden called Linden. I have no memory of the Oliver Street house. But when I was three, we moved into my grandmother's house at 96 Belmont St. Belmont Street constituted the city line; across the street was the despised city of Everett--a low and vulgar place, in contrast to our elegant Malden, we all understood. I remember this three-story place very well. There were eight of us--my mother, my father, my two sisters, my grandmother, my two aunts and me--packed into a house with three bedrooms, a finished attic and one bath. Then another sister (Mary) was born in 1948 and then another (Patty) in 1950. Cozy.

The house at 96 Belmont St., Malden. Photo taken in the 1970s.
My sister Ann and Aunt May on the front steps.

I loved the house. I especially loved my grandmother whom I called "Nana." She was soft and cuddly. She adored me and never rebuked or disciplined me. In 1949, when I was four, she and Aunts May and Kay took me on a long train trip from Boston to Tampa, Fla. to attend the United Spanish American War Veterans convention. (Her husband, the late John Perry, had served in that war.) I had a grand time. I'm told--though I don't recall doing this--that I entertained people in the hotel bar where we stayed by telling risqué jokes. "Did you hear about the two flies on the toilet seat?" went the joke. "One got pissed off." General hilarity.

In those ancient days, you still had street vendors and milkmen plying the streets of Malden. The milk came in thick glass bottles, including chocolate milk except when--on a signal from my mother--the milkman would explain to me sadly that the "chocolate cow was sick today." There was a "ragman" who came by in a pushcart to pick up discarded cloths and another guy who sharpened knives and scissors. Another who brought a little pony and a cowboy outfit that I donned and was photographed sitting atop the pony. My favorite was the Italian organ grinder who was accompanied by a trained monkey. The Italian guy would push his contraption on big colorful wheels in front of your house and start playing and you'd come out and applaud and the monkey, wearing an embroidered vest and hat, would take off the hat and scamper around collecting coins in his hat in payment. And everyone would laugh and clap for the monkey too.

On the front steps of 96 Belmont St. Back row (L to R): Brenda, Ann, Mary,
Nana. Front row (L to R): me, Aunt Kay, Aunt May. November 1948.

Back yard of 96 Belmont St. (L to R): me, my mother, Nana, Mary, Brenda, my father. Summer 1949.

I get to ride the pony. Malden, Probably 1949.

96 Belmont St. was just a quick 15-minute bus ride away from Revere Beach, reputedly the first public beach in the United States, a fabulous two-mile long stretch of bright yellow sand along the Atlantic Ocean. The water was clean and cold. And in the 1940s, the waterfront offered a dazzling assortment of restaurants, ice cream parlors, custard shops, amusements and rides: "flying horses," fun houses, bumper cars, shooting galleries and an enormous and heart-stopping and dangerous roller-coaster--"The Cyclone." We'd drive there as a family on weekends. Sometimes Ann--who was 12 in 1949--would take Brenda (age ten) and me (age four) and we'd travel by bus all by ourselves to Revere Beach. My mother would smear us with olive oil (!) to protect us from the sun (!) and would make us baloney and cheese sandwiches with French's Mustard on white bread; we'd carry these with us to the beach. To me, the ocean always smelled of olive oil and baloney and cheese and French's Mustard.

Revere Beach. Summer 1948. (L to R): Ann, my mother, Brenda, me, Aunt May.

People were constantly dropping in to visit at 96 Belmont St. My parents loved to entertain. My mother would play the piano and lead everyone in singing. They served beer and rye whiskey and red wine mixed with ginger ale. My father liked to drink; my mother did not. They had lots of friends. Everyone liked Charlie and Peg. My mother's Uncle Dan, tall and elegant with silver hair was often there with his white dog, Tappy. My parents had loads of old high school friends who had stayed around Malden--the "gang," they called them. And there were lots of veterans now who had come back from the War. The house was always full of people and it was merry.

We visited other people too. My mother seemed to have an infinite number of aunts. It was a special treat to visit her Aunt Helen (and cousins Ginny and Honey) who lived in a magical place: a sprawling jumble of a house perched on a high precipice above the ocean in the town of Marblehead. The house offered an enormous enclosed front porch with banks of windows around three sides affording stunning views of the sea from Naugus Point. The porch was hung with the most fantastic and implausible decorations: huge conch shells and the skulls of sharks and cutlasses fashioned from whales' teeth. You stepped from this porch onto a narrow terrace and found yourself high above a rocky inlet and tiny beach to which you could descend--carefully--by a vertiginous, 100-foot stairway cut into the face of the cliff fitted with a comforting metal handrail. The waves surged far below.

Outside the house in Marblehead. Summer 1949. My mother holding Mary with her uncle, Fr. Francis Lucey, SJ, Rector of the Georgetown University School of Law.

TELEVISION

We were the first people in our neighborhood to get a television set. All the neighbors came over to watch. This was 1948. The first show I ever saw was a newscast with John Cameron Swayze of NBC News. At first we put the TV on the stove in the kitchen. Or am I confusing this with that stupid joke about setting the TV on the stove so that people could watch "Milton Boil!"

Everybody loved the Milton Berle Show which came on at 8 o'clock on Tuesdays. It was a variety show with singers and leggy dancers. But mostly it was Berle who was an outlandish vaudeville comedian doing vulgar impressions and slapstick. Here was a favorite: whenever anyone said the word "makeup" in the course of a skit--for example, someone says to Berle, "I'm sorry we had this argument, we should MAKE UP!"--a stooge would come running from the wings with a huge can of makeup powder and smack Berle in the face with a giant puff duster producing a great cloud of powder. It was a scream!

My older sisters, Ann and Brenda, had previously been radio fans--they loved scary shows like "The Shadow"--and they had tried to get me to listen too. But once the TV appeared, I would have none of it. And soon they abandoned their radio dramas and we all became TV nuts. Everyone did, even though in 1948 there were only two television stations in Boston and TV programming didn't come on the air until 3 o'clock in the afternoon. I vividly remember sitting with Ann and Brenda in front of our TV, by then located in our basement, staring at the motionless test pattern on the set as the minutes ticked down to 3 o'clock when one of the afternoon westerns would begin. My mother came down to the basement with a load of laundry and found us there, transfixed by the motionless, silent TV screen. "What are you kids looking at?" she said, amazed at our paralytic stupidity. "We're waiting for the cowboy movie to begin," we explained.

I had my favorite shows: "Keukla, Fran and Ollie" starring the affable, none-too-bright single-toothed dragon, Keukla; "Ding, Dong School" with the wonderful teacher, Miss Francis. And best of all, "The Howdy Doody Show" starring Howdy himself--a freckled-faced puppet--and two other puppets, the grumpy Mr. Bluster and the beautiful Indian maiden, Princess Summer-Fall-Winter-Spring, and two humans, the avuncular Buffalo Bob Smith and the silly clown, Clarabelle. How I envied the lucky kids who got be on the Howdy Doody Show and actually were able to sit in the Peanut Gallery! The best I got to do was to wear my Howdy Doody tie to church now and then.

There were other shows I loved to watch. "Andy's Gang" on Saturday mornings provided an ongoing serial usually set in India or in some other exotic location. The best thing about this show, however, was not the serial itself, but the chuckling introductions by the master of ceremonies, old cowboy sidekick, Andy Devine. Andy was accompanied by two astounding characters. There was Midnight the Cat, who seemed able to play a steam pipe organ and who would turn slowly to the audience while playing and purr, "Niiice!" I thought for years that Midnight was a real cat. And there was Froggy the Gremlin, a rubbery reptilian who appeared on top of a grandfather clock on the set, and who sparred with Andy and with the audience in a smartass, sarcastic repartee--"Hiya kids, hiya, hiya!" he'd smirk--and finally disappear in a flash and cloud of smoke while Andy shouted lewdly, "Plunk your magic twanger, Froggie!" It was transcendent!

And there were great cowboy movies on TV, recycled old Westerns, mostly B-films made in the 1930s and 40s now trundled out to fill in the empty television hours. Largely forgotten stars from 20 years earlier like Hoot Gibson and Ken Maynard and Lash LaRue were suddenly all over TV. The biggest of them all was Hopalong Cassidy, who not only revived the slew of films he had made in the 30s, but now started making new ones explicitly for TV. He still looked terrific. In fact he looked better, probably because he resembled Eisenhower. "Hoppy" was my favorite cowboy. Once I started school I got a Hopalong Cassidy lunchbox and Hopalong Cassidy savings bank (you put the coins in a slot in his ten gallon hat) and a Hopalong Cassidy read-along record book, "The Singing Bandit."

CATHOLICISM

Being Roman Catholic was an essential, defining element in my family's understanding of its identity. That, and being Irish. The two went together.

We were Catholic because we were Irish; it never occurred to me that we were also "Scottish" or (God forbid) "English." We were Catholic because we possessed the will and the discipline to go to church every single Sunday, not like those indolent Protestants, and because we went to confession on Saturday. We were Catholic, of course, because my father's brother, Albert--"Father Al"--was a priest, and so was my mother's Uncle Frank--not only a priest, mind you, but the regent of Georgetown Law School, Fr. Francis Lucey, S.J. And we were Catholic like all our closest friends in Malden--like my uncle's wife, Emma, who went to the "French" church and the Italians like Bruce Chatzi and his wife and the Morgantis, part of the regular gang that congregated at the house. All these emigrant coreligionists were bound together in perceived common suffering with the Irish because they had all been denigrated and deplored by the once-majority Anglo-Protestants who used to rule the Boston roost and whose tyranny continued to be the lore of the stories I heard around the house.

How the WASP teachers wouldn't let the Catholic kids out of class for Good Friday services or Holy Days of Obligation--until (in my mother's telling) her father stormed the principal's office and rescued the hostage children. How Protestant merchants hung their "INNA" signs in their shop windows--"Irish Need Not Apply"--turning away immigrant job seekers in the first years of the 20th century, condemning them to crushing poverty. How we always, in response, displayed a small framed photo of Archbishop Cushing in our house--as though he were a member of the family--an Irish cleric protector there to slay Protestant intruders. This was a tribe that relished the avenging triumph of James Michael Curley when he became mayor of Boston in the face of aristocratic opposition. He was a rogue, certainly, but he was our score-settling rogue. And, of course, we would all fall in love with the Irish-Catholic, John Fitzgerald Kennedy, who defeated the Protestant blue-blood, Henry Cabot Lodge, to become senator from Massachusetts in 1952. Sweet retributive justice.

I wonder if this sense of being a member of an oppressed minority inclined my mother to feel sympathy for and solidarity with the Jews she knew in Malden. The city had a diverse population--though there were virtually no blacks there in the 1940s and 50s. I look today through a 1953 reunion roster for my mother's high school class of 1933 and see that of 134 graduates, 20 (15%) had surnames that suggest an ethnic-Jewish background: Bluestein, Greenbaum, Weintraub, Sugarman, Shenfield, Hurwitz, etc. My mother knew these people. Did she regard them as outsiders like herself? Did this lead her later to choose a Jewish doctor--the redoubtable Dr. Solomon--to deliver her children? And at the end of her life, did it predispose her to find her best friend in the Jewish Sid Rosenthal?

In any case, our family's Catholicism--its *Irish* Catholicism--went deep. It's not surprising that we felt a strong attraction to and loyalty for Boston College, which was a Jesuit university and which pulsed with Boston and Irish sanctimoniousness. My sister Ann would graduate from BC. Ann and Brenda would marry BC graduates named McGuiggin and Murphy. It was not surprising that my mother, the pianist, would become a church organist in a Catholic church. It was inevitable that I would become an altar boy once I turned 12. I had no choice. It was just as clear, however, that I should not become a priest because my mother possessed a clear-eyed, sober assessment of how priests--especially parish priests--conducted their lives, and she was not much impressed. They always drank too much, she thought. We remember Fr. Bernie Harvey--long-time friend of the family--showing up blind drunk at my parents' house with some regularity.

The Catholicism we practiced was all about rituals and rules: attending Mass, going to confession, fasting before communion, genuflecting before the altar, repeating the prayers one memorized in the prescribed order. Beyond obeying these rules and observing these norms, we didn't talk much about personal behavior or conscience. How was one supposed to act toward other people? How was one supposed to be a *good* person? We never discussed ethical or moral matters. We never entertained the question of what it meant to be a Christian. I don't think it ever occurred to me that we *were* Christians. We were not Christians; we were Catholics.

And my mother's chip-on-the-shoulder Irish-Catholic combativeness was quick to boil over. Once, when I was about nine or ten, I had the temerity to inform her that I had learned that the Roman Catholic Church was the largest single religious organization in both the United States and the world--I had always until then imagined that we were a tiny minority in an enormous Protestant sea. She turned on me furiously and snapped "Who told you that!" I could only sputter that I had encountered this truth in a book somewhere, but she clearly regarded me as having betrayed a tribal pact.

MUSIC

In Malden I used to listen to the old Victrola record player that my grandmother owned. She had a collection of ancient 78 RPM records, so old they were recorded only on one side. Those 78s were so heavy and fragile, they'd break even if you dropped them on one of her lush oriental rugs.

My father had a big record collection--again, all 78s which were the only things that existed in those days. He liked Bing Crosby ("Mares eat oats/And does eat oats/And little lambs eat ivy/A kid'll eat ivy too/Wouldn't you!") and Vaughn Monroe ("Moon over Miami") and the Mills Brothers, and the Andrew Sisters, and Fred Waring and the Pennsylvanians. There were some light classics: Strauss Waltzes and a recording of Rhapsody in Blue with Morton Gould at the piano that became a favorite of mine.

My real knowledge of music began in the early 50s when I was six and seven years old as I would listen with Ann and Brenda to their hit tunes on the radio. In the summertime, when we were on vacation from school, the radio was on all day. I learned all the songs and knew all the words. These were ballads and love songs and dance tunes and goofy novelty songs. They were wonderful.

There was Jo Stafford singing "You Belong to Me" ("Fly the ocean in a silver plane/See the jungle when it's wet with rain."); Eddie Fisher doing "Wish You Were Here" ("They're not making the sky so blue this year/Wish you were here."); Patti Page mugging her way through "How Much is That Doggie in the Window?" ("The one with the waggily tail/Arf, arf!"); Or the Four Aces belting out "Standin' on the Corner Watchin' All the Girls Go By" (Standin' on the corner givin' all the girls the eye."). There was that Korean War weeper by Jean Shepard and Ferlin Husky, "Dear John" ("Dear John/ Oh, how I hate to write!"). Or, still my favorite, Doris Day as Calamity Jane singing "Secret Love" ("Once I had a secret love/That lived within the heart of me.")

All this was before rock and roll, before Bill Haley and His Comets in 1954 and Elvis in 1956. By then my foundational musical tastes had already been shaped. The mold was set. At bottom, I liked show tunes and ballads--pretty corny, conventional stuff, pretty old-fashioned stuff for a ten-year old at the dawn of a new musical era. I would go on to love a lot of rock. But I couldn't let go of all those patterns that had been set in the early 1950s. I wouldn't let go of Doris Day.

MOVIES

I think the first movie I saw was "Bambi," probably when I was three years old in 1948. I loved it, but it was scary. Parents were always being lost in those Disney films. And then we saw "Cinderella" which came out in 1950: much better, not scary. And then "Pinocchio."

I was entranced and puzzled by those movie theaters: I thought the small silhouetted figures sitting way down front near the screen were dwarfs. My father once on an impulse took me to see "The Secret Lives of Walter Mitty" with Danny Kaye and Virginia Mayo. We were walking by the Granada Theater in downtown Malden--it was probably 1948 because the movie was made in 1947--and when he saw it was playing there, he decided on the spot that we should go in, just he and I. But he failed to tell my mother, of course, who became frantic when we didn't come home on time and then she became furious with his casual, unapologetic explanation that it was just something he felt like doing.

After we moved to Burlington, there were no more casual drop-ins at the Granada. There were no movie theaters at all in Burlington. Occasionally we'd go to nearby Woburn to see a movie and more rarely into Boston itself. It was probably in Woburn that I saw "Hans Christian Anderson," again with Danny Kaye, with its marvelous score and terrific songs that I loved to sing: "Wonderful, Wonderful, Copenhagen!" "Anywhere I Wander," "Ugly Duckling," "Inchworm." And it was probably in Woburn that we saw another great musical from that period, "White Christmas," with Bing Crosby, with Danny Kaye (again) and Rosemary Clooney, (George's aunt) and Vera Ellen. In the summer of 1953, when I was eight, and my parents were visiting Father Al, in Canada, they left Brenda and me at home with Ann to look after us. (I'm not sure where five-year-old Mary and three-year-old Patty were.) Ann took Brenda and me into Boston on the bus to see the sensational science fiction hit, "The War of the Worlds." It was fabulous. And it scared the hell out of all three of us. I wouldn't dare go upstairs alone when we got back to the empty house because I was terrified I'd encounter one of those trifocal Martian periscopes that came out of their spaceships on long tentacles.

I really only began to see lots of movies when they started to appear on television in the mid-1950s. The Hollywood studios had initially resisted allowing their films to be shown on TV because they feared the competition from television. But in February 1956, Jack Warner sold the rights to all of Warner Brothers pre-1950 films to television distributors and then the floodgates opened. The other studios followed. Suddenly all the classic films from the 30s, 40s, and then into the 50s as well were appearing on late night and afternoon TV. It was all free. The ABC station in Boston created "Cinema 7" at 3 o'clock on Sunday afternoons. The first film they showed was "High Noon" with Gary Cooper and Grace Kelly, then "Laura" with Dana Andrews and Gene Tierney, then "Sahara" with Humphrey Bogart. These were significant cultural events, it seemed. In the spring of 1956, "The Wizard of Oz" from 1939 appeared on prime-time TV on a Saturday evening. It was stunning, even if, on our black and white television, Dorothy did not step into a Technicolor Munchkinland when she and Toto first opened the door of their wrecked Kansas farmhouse.

There was suddenly a Late Show every night on some channel with a classic film; some were good, some weren't. It was haphazard, but they were all there. I treasured these movies, and came to believe that they were important, that they represented something genuine and authentic about American art and life. You had to *know* about this stuff. And the movie stars! I met Clark Gable and Bette Davis and Henry Fonda and Katherine Hepburn and Tyrone Power and Olivia de Havilland and Spencer Tracy and Claudette Colbert and Ann Sheridan. I learned all their names. All these larger-than-life creations of the studio system. And, of course, I met the most compelling one of them all: Errol Flynn.

ERROL FLYNN

Errol Flynn made 35 films for Warner Brothers between 1935 and 1952. I saw nearly all of them on television by the time I was 15 and I loved them.

Flynn's movies vary widely: war films, lots of Westerns, historical romances and dramas, a few screwball comedies. Some are better than others. He's remembered above all for a handful of spectacular adventure films created over a five-year span from 1935 to 1940 in which he soared as the most dazzling swashbuckler the movies ever produced: "Captain Blood," "The Charge of the Light Brigade," "The Prince and the Pauper," "The Adventures of Robin Hood," "The Sea Hawk." These films boasted magnificent original scores written by Erich Wolfgang Korngold and Max Steiner, late romantic Hollywood movie music at its very best.

These are irresistible movies, and I did not attempt to resist. Why was I so taken by Flynn? It was his grace and athleticism and intelligence and flippant charm, I think. I relished his easy wit, his *sprezzatura*, his buoyant "English" presence, so different from the loutish John Wayne, for example. Here was a model of effortless male competence and sexual self-assurance. He was elegant and cool.

He played marvelous characters. There were gallant soldiers, dashing officers: the doomed George Armstrong Custer; the doomed Earl of Essex whom the queen he loves will send to the block; the unjustly condemned Peter Blood who will become a pirate and restore his honor; the soldier of fortune, Miles Hendon, who saves the boy king, Edward VI, from the conspiracies of the traitorous Earl of Hertford; Major Geoffrey Vickers, the heroic British cavalry officer who leads his regiment into the Russian cannonade at Balaclava; Don Juan, the great Spanish lover who rescues his queen from the machinations of the wicked first minister. And, of course, he is Robin Hood. But in all of these roles and all the others, he was first and always Errol Flynn: impossibly good looking, winking at a camera that loved him and the fluency with which he moved.

Flynn may not have been a great actor. But Richard Schickel chooses Flynn--not Bogart, not Tracy, not Cooper, not Frederic March--as his favorite film actor of the 1930s and 40s in part because there was much to be said for "the grace and ease of a man who was never caught acting." And Flynn was capable of good performances. He is moving and understated in "The Dawn Patrol" as the tragic pilot who must take command of his sacrificial fighter squadron in the midst of a meaningless war. He has an agonizing scene in "Operation Burma" when he must recover a fellow soldier who has been tortured by the Japanese. And in his last big budget feature for Warner Brothers, "The Adventures of Don Juan," he portrays the great aging lover in a bit of gentle self-parody that is a treasure to watch.

Maybe I liked Flynn because I was just a kid and, as David Thomson says, Flynn had "a freshness, a galvanizing energy, a cheerful gaiety (in the old sense) made to inspire boys."

BURLINGTON

In the summer of 1950 we moved from my grandmother's house on Belmont Street in Malden. This happened very suddenly and it was not a pleasant parting. I didn't understand then why we were moving or that there was so much animosity associated with the departure. We were crowded in that house, of course. I understand now that there was unhappiness on the part of my grandmother and aunts when my mother had a fifth child (Patty) in early 1950. Ann tells me now that there were serious disputes over money between my grandmother and aunts, on the one hand, and my father and mother, on the other. In any case, relations became bitter and the rupture was deep. I loved my grandmother and was close to her, but after we left that June, I wouldn't see her for 15 years although we lived only a half hour away.

Years later, my mother told me that in 1948--about the time our family moved into Belmont Street with my grandmother and aunts--my grandfather, Albert MacDonald, died and left his house in Malden to my father. This was an opportunity, said my mother, for us to have a house of our own. But my father sold his father's house and my mother told me he would not explain to her what he had done with the money--something on the order of a handsome $8,000: about $85,800 in 2019 dollars. It was *his* money, not hers, he told her.

In any case, in 1950 we moved from the contested Belmont Street to the town of Burlington, a different world. Malden was urban, filled with houses, streetcars, buses, and people--59,804 of them. Burlington in 1950 was empty--just 3,250 inhabitants. The boondocks.

And the place we moved into represented an astonishing change from where we had been living. It was my mother's Aunt Catherine's "summer house" which she agreed to rent to us. We found ourselves in a sprawling, rambling place with an attached empty apartment and a very large detached barn that had probably once sheltered animals. There was lots of land including a big front yard with huge oak trees. There were pear trees in the enormous back yard that terminated in a forest. Across the street, behind a tumbledown stonewall, was a neglected apple orchard and beyond the orchard, blueberry patches. Everything about the property was overgrown and wild. The house was expansive but primitive. No running water in the sink in the kitchen--you had to use a hand pump. No refrigerator--it was, literally, an icebox, with a large block of ice delivered weekly by, yes, the iceman. The stove in the kitchen took coal. No heat on the second floor, and no insulation up there either. People weren't supposed to be living there in winter.

And it was awful in winter on that second floor. You ran up the stairs and jumped into those freezing beds and wrapped yourself in as many layers of blankets as you could. After a couple of years, we got electric blankets which saved us.

I kind of liked the place. There was a rude calm about it and a naturalness that was beguiling to a little boy. Those pear trees right in the back yard! You wrested the pears from the high branches with long bamboo poles that had little wire cages on the end which you fitted round the pears and then shook gently until the tree yielded up the fruit. And we'd hang empty coffee cans on strings around our necks and pick blueberries in the big low blueberry patch that ranged past the apple orchard across the street. The blueberries fell in--ping, ping, ping. In the middle of the patch were six- and seven-foot-high dun-colored ant hills. Scary and surreal. The woods were filled with small ponds that exploded with tadpoles in spring. There were enormous spiders and surreptitious, angry yellowjackets everywhere. Brenda accidentally kicked over one of those yellowjacket nests one time as we were walking in the woods and the wasps chased and stung us furiously. It was a fearsome and wonderful place.

We five kids spent a lot of time together in Burlington. Ann was just short of her 13th birthday when we moved there in June 1950; Brenda was not quite 11. I was five. Mary was just two and Patty was only five months old. Patty was pink and unbearably cute and easy to be with. Mary was passionate and emotional and intense. I don't remember playing much with Mary and Patty when they were little girls. When, after about two years, my mother went back to full-time work, we had to enlist the help of a neighbor to look after Mary and Patty because the rest of us were in school. (Later, I think I specialized in annoying Mary and Patty with pedantic current-affairs quizzes around the breakfast table which they always failed. They found me, I'm sure, extremely annoying.) In those early years in Burlington, much of the supervision of the younger kids fell to Ann. She was very good at this because she was smart, even-tempered and good-humored. She was a realist; she was like my mother. We believed what she told us. In the summer of 1954, when she was going into her senior year in high school, Ann went to live with our dentist and his wife, Paul and Lorraine Sheeran, in nearby Woburn where she took care of their three young children even as she continued to complete her schooling. We all missed her terribly.

On the front lawn in Burlington, probably summer 1953. Back row (L to R): Mary, Ann (holding one of the Morganti kids), Brenda. Front row (L to R): me, Frankie Morganti, his brother, Patty.

If Ann was a realist, Brenda preferred fiction. She loved telling stories about miracles and the amazing events associated with the appearances of saints and martyrs. She especially favored stories about stigmata, about holy statues that bled from their orifices. She was my partner in fantasies. One time she and I practiced performing together in our big barn (where the acoustics were favorable) the then popular Christmas song "I Saw Mama Kissing Santa Claus," and Brenda announced that the results were so excellent that we should inform my mother that it was our intention to go into show business. Brenda determined that I was the one to convey this information to my mother. I did. She received the news quietly and with little enthusiasm.

Brenda, Patty, Mary. Burlington. Summer 1954. .

I DISCOVER WORLD WAR II

Beginning in the fall of 1952, when I was seven, NBC TV started broadcasting "Victory at Sea," a 26-part weekly documentary history of naval operations during the Second World War. Each 30-minute episode was dramatically crafted from (mostly) authentic documentary film, assembled into fluent and coherent story lines presided over by the authoritative narrative voice of Leonard Graves. The episodes had resonant, weighty titles indicating their gravity and import: "Fire on the Waters," "The Magnetic North," "Mare Nostrum," "Mediterranean Mosaic" and so on. Most significantly, the series had a magnificent original score composed to accompany the TV show by Richard Rogers, the composer of the Broadway hits "Oklahoma," "Carousel" and "South Pacific." Rogers's music for "Victory at Sea" was exquisite: lyrical and deeply moving. "Victory at Sea" was great television--maybe the first great television show. It came on at 10 o'clock on Friday night. Since it was a Friday, I was permitted stay up to watch. The program affected me deeply. Seven years after the war ended, seven years after my birth, I discovered World War II. It seemed to me, in those gripping black and white images and Graves's powerful baritone and that enthralling score, that World War II was the most important and the most interesting thing that had ever happened--so much more important and interesting and compelling than anything else in everyday life or in school. It was all I wanted to talk about or read about.

We had about that time acquired a set of the World Book Encyclopedia (my father had sold them briefly and unsuccessfully) and I read everything I could find about World War II in those volumes. When I'd exhausted that source and clamored for more, I recall my mother and father hesitating and exchanging uncertain looks and then, finally, my father proceeding to a large closet in the living room and retrieving from a deep place on a high shelf a treasure which they were evidently unsure I was ready to receive. But now he placed before me five handsome, faux-leather, black-bound volumes set in a heavy custom-made bookstand: "Pictorial History of the Second World War." There it was! I had in my hands, as the subtitle succinctly expressed, "a photographic record of all theaters of action chronologically arranged." Beginning September 3, 1939 with a picture of Neville Chamberlain reading the declaration of war against Germany and continuing through the war crimes trials in the fall of 1946, 2505 pages of photographs--the pages were numbered consecutively over the five volumes--each with a brief explanatory text for virtually every day of the war and the first year after. The whole war!

One of those photographs had a particularly profound effect on me. On facing pages 2130 and 2131 in Volume V, I encountered a photograph described as "A Page From Hitler's Book." The caption under the photo read: *"THE NAZIS IN WARSAW. This photograph, depicting the Nazis 'cleaning out' the Ghetto in Warsaw, Poland, was presented in evidence at the Nuremberg Trial. The photograph is a copy from a leather-bound book which contained the report of the German commander who was responsible for the Nazi acts in the Warsaw Ghetto. Women and children are herded before the Nazi firearms."* The picture is now a famous one. On the left-hand side of the photo, a group of civilians--women and men and children--move toward the camera with their arms raised. The woman in front is turning to look to her left. On the right-hand side of the photograph--where the woman is looking--there are German soldiers in helmets. An SS man stands at the ready casually holding a machine pistol and stares at the camera. In the foreground, very close, a little boy (my age) with his hands up, walks unsteadily, slightly apart from the rest of the group. He is frightened.

Nazis "cleaning out" the Warsaw Ghetto. May 1943.

The photograph puzzled and upset me. Obviously something very bad was happening to these people. I turned to my mother and asked her why the photographer did not intervene to help them. I imagined that the photographer must represent some benign, independent agency, and that in witnessing and recording this moment, he must wish to do even more; he must want to step into this drama unfolding before him and rescue these innocent and endangered people. My mother explained that the photographer was, in fact, one of the Nazis himself. I was stunned. The photographer was witnessing a very evil thing and he approved of it and wanted to record it so that other people could see it too. How could he not understand that this was evil? How could he approve of this? But he was glad the little boy was frightened. He was glad the boy was going to be murdered. More than that, he wanted to take pictures of it. I think at one level I became a historian at that moment. I needed to try to plumb this mystery, to grasp how it was possible for human beings to do immeasurably cruel things and to be proud of doing these things. Believing, apparently, that they are doing good things when they are doing very bad things.

I started immediately to read all five volumes of the "Pictorial History." One page at a time; one photograph at a time. I learned everything about the war from those books. I knew the outcome of every battle, the name of every airplane, the designation of every tank, the rank of every officer, the design of every uniform. I took the books to school--third grade, mind you--and the teachers let me give presentations to the class. I'd hold up the books and show the pictures and tell the other kids what the pictures meant. I must have been insufferable. Why didn't they beat me up?

LEARNING THE WRONG LESSONS

I just said that I learned everything about the Second World War from that pictorial history which my parents commended into my hands with some hesitancy when I was about eight years old.

I learned too much, actually. I became deeply, narrowly, obsessively absorbed in the subject of the War. My interest and knowledge of the War crowded out other things. I became contemptuous of other subjects and of other people who were interested in those other subjects and who did not share my passion and expertise. And it seemed, no one else really did. I was singular and isolated in that expertise. And even with respect to the War, the truth was that I had learned, or imagined that I had learned, far more than I actually knew. This bred a breezy insouciance and arrogance.

I'm looking at a document from the spring of 1955, a list of oral book reports I gave before my fifth grade class that year. I see among the 10 books listed, the titles "The Eastern Front" and "North Africa" by someone named "Pyle." (presumably the famous war correspondent, Ernie Pyle). Neither of these books existed; I must have made them up. I see that I also list "Pictorial History of the Second World War." It certainly did exist, but it was not written by "Pyle" as I assert in my report. These frauds went undetected by my credulous classmates and by dear Mrs. Burgess, our teacher.

I had become a phony and a faker. A bullshitter. I had come to think that I already knew it all and that everyone else was a dope. I had come to believe that further reading was unnecessary. Additional study was optional. I could bluff my way through.

It would take me too long to unlearn that lesson.

SCHOOL

I asked earlier why my friends in the third grade hadn't beaten me up when I subjected them to what must have been my insufferable lectures. They probably didn't beat me up because we all knew each other and we were all friends. There was only one elementary school in tiny Burlington--the Union School--and there was only one class in each grade, so you were always with the same kids as you progressed each year from one grade to the next. We had known each other since the first grade. We all understood our foibles and idiosyncrasies and we were all more or less nice to each other. It was the 1950s.

So here I am with my buddies at my eighth birthday party in March 1953 when I was in the third grade. That's me kneeling in front, second from the left, wearing a tie which my mother thought appropriate for the occasion (the other mothers evidently did not). My best friend was Paul Gurney, standing second from left. He was big and popular and athletic. Next to him, third from left, is Eddie Nolan, smart and witty. And kneeling next to me, first on the left, is John Malatesta, a lively, sincere boy. I remember the others but have lost their names. They liked the pictures I knew how to draw and the stories and jokes I knew how to tell from the TV shows I watched.

My eighth birthday party. Burlington. March 1953

I did well in school but it didn't excite me. I have my report card from the third grade and see that I got an "A" for the year in English, reading, spelling, and penmanship and a "B" in mathematics. In music, drawing, science, health, effort, conduct, and homework I received an "S," "Satisfactory." One either got "Satisfactory" or "Unsatisfactory." There was no history or any kind of social studies taught in the third grade, so it's not surprising I was bored.

Once my mother started back to work in 1952-53, our pre-school ritual was highly-structured and unyielding. She left the house for Boston extremely early in the morning. My father drifted off about then as well. Ann was in charge. She'd get little Mary and Patty down the street to the neighbor who looked after them during the day. Then she and Brenda would be off in the bus for high school about 7:30. That left me alone. I was seven or eight years old. I'd sit in the kitchen, fully dressed, with my coat and hat on, holding my lunchbox, watching an alarm clock set for 8 o'clock. When the alarm sounded, I'd turn it off, take my lunch box, leave the house, turn right, walk to the end of Chestnut Avenue, turn right again up Wilmington Street., walk about 100 yards to the big municipal barn where the school bus was located and wait there for the bus driver. I was his first passenger every day. We became friends.

BURLINGTON GOES BAD

Sometime after the first couple of years in Burlington, things began to go wrong there. It was probably mortifying for my mother to have been exiled to Burlington in the first place. The house lacked the 20th century amenities to which she was accustomed in Malden. Her social networks had been stretched, if not broken. And then we became poor.

My father and I. Burlington 1953. One of us appears to be dressed for church.

Around 1952 my father lost his job as office manager at Jurgeson Gage and Valve. My mother tells me that he'd started drinking during lunch and then simply stopped coming back to work. She called Mr. Jurgeson himself and pleaded that my father be kept on, and Jurgeson apparently tried to help, but my father spiraled out of control. Ann tells me she learned from my mother that finally he simply put a piece of paper in his typewriter and wrote "I Quit" and walked out. From there he drifted from one job to another--mostly sales, some door-to-door stuff including selling encyclopedias--the World Book. But he gradually fell apart and didn't work at all. By the summer of 1954, he would sit in one of the Adirondack chairs on our lawn, unkempt and sometimes unshaven, drinking beer in the afternoon, listening to sentimental records--the "Ballad of Little Jimmy Brown" was a favorite--sometimes calling my mother at work and pestering her with long maudlin soliloquies. I was nine and this was sad to observe. He was only 41, but he was a broken man and he was losing his marriage and his family.

How to explain? Why do people fall apart? What defeated him? Was the professional competition more than he could acknowledge? My mother told me that he complained about the "college boys" he encountered in the office with baccalaureate degrees--he had only a two-year degree from a business school. Was he nagged by a sense of not having fulfilled his duty during the war? We had all those strange photos of him posing in uniforms--American and Canadian. Did he berate himself in retrospect for not having served during World War II? Did he feel somehow unworthy? I never asked him.

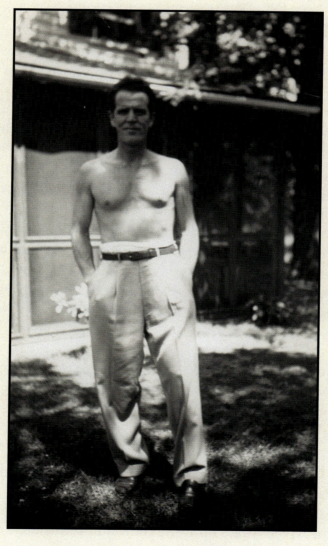

My father in decline. Burlington 1954.

In any case, we began running out of money and you could see the signs. One day a bill collector came to the house. My mother recognized what he was as he crossed the big lawn. She grabbed Patty and Mary and me and pulled us under one of the windows beside the front porch and told us not to make a sound. The bill collector knocked on the front door for a long time and peered in the windows--right over our heads where we crouched. Finally convinced there was nobody home, he left. And at Christmas 1952, I received a gift--a battlefield game of soldiers and tanks--that was obviously ancient and was missing pieces. Someone had made heroic and loving efforts to clean the thing up and refit this relic, but it simply didn't work right. I think I was worried by this omen.

Then our cars stopped working. And then they disappeared entirely and we had to rely on buses. My father would occasionally buy an old clunker--I recall one particularly hideous pre-war, powder blue contraption that sported a heavy cord that draped behind the front seat which you were supposed to use to pull yourself out of the cavernous rear seat that gobbled up the unwary. My mother regarded this machine with disdain and refused to enter. "Oh, Charlie," she said pityingly, and walked away. The car lasted about two days.

As my father disintegrated, my mother came fully into her own and asserted her independence and authority. She was an extraordinarily willful and self-possessed woman, a force of nature. And she was prepared to move on past Charlie MacDonald, which he did not realize until too late.

At some point after Patty was born in 1950, when my mother was 35, she decided she didn't want to have any more children--at least, not with him. My father wanted more children, apparently because he wished to have another son, and so he pressed my mother to continue. But she objected that five kids was enough; moreover, they didn't have the money to support the kids they had so why should they have more. My father sought a theological ally in this disputation and recruited his brother, Father Al, who at some point came down from Canada where he lived and argued--gently, though persistently--that it was my mother's duty, as a good Catholic wife, to submit to her husband and to continue to procreate. But my mother had a theological ally too--in the powerful person of her uncle Frank, provost of the Georgetown School of Law. Fr. Frank Lucey, SJ assured my mother that five children constituted more than adequate demonstration of her piety and that she needed to protect her health. If she didn't want to have any more children with Charlie MacDonald, said Fr. Lucey, that was okay with the Pope.

The question quickly became academic because my mother had no time to have more children. When my father's career fell apart, my mother realized she had to go back to work. We had no money. So she resumed the kind of work she had done for the federal government and had stopped in 1945 when I was born. My mother had earned a degree in commercial art from the Massachusetts School of Art after high school, and during World War II she had used this preparatory education to develop the skills of a technical draftsperson. Beginning in 1952-53, she took a job, first at an engineering firm in Boston, Charles T. Main, Inc., to which she commuted every day by bus, and then at Hanscom Air Force Base in nearby Bedford. She would continue that work for the next nearly 30 years until she retired in 1980 at age 65.

JOE HURLEY

As the consequences of my father's alcoholism became more evident and he lost one job after another, my mother turned for assistance to the parish priests she knew at St. Margaret's Church in Burlington where she worked as organist for Sunday Masses. This brought Joseph Hurley--then Fr. Joseph Hurley--into our lives in 1953.

He was tall--about 6'1"--outlandishly good-looking and immaculately dressed in his black clerical suit when I first saw him at our house. Black hair brushed back. Beautifully shaven, smelling of cologne. Thirty-three years old, five years younger than my mother. An Irish-Catholic priest. He had come to talk to my father, to counsel him, to persuade him to stop drinking and return to the bosom of his family. A scene from a soap opera.

Joe Hurley. Summer 1955.

I have no idea when he and my mother started sleeping together. By the fall of 1954, Joe had left the priesthood and was teaching high school English somewhere and my mother and I were visiting him at his house in Winchester on Saturday afternoons. I was being cautioned to keep silent about these episodes with the password, "Mum's the word." I relished being in on the secret. I liked Joe. He was competent and handsome. He drove a car that worked--it was actually a Cadillac. He brought bags of food to the house that included individually-wrapped parcels of thin-sliced ham and turkey and Swiss cheese from a delicatessen, something I'd never seen before.

When did my father figure out what was going on between his wife and the (ex)priest? Here's a scene. In the spring of 1954, when I was nine, I was promoted from the minor league Little League team, The Flying Saucers, to the major league, Marvin Brothers, team. This was clearly an error, because I was a terrible player. But I was very pleased, because I got to exchange the crummy Flying Saucers yellow tee-shirt uniform for a full grey-flannel Marvin Brothers uniform with black and red trim that resembled the uniform of the Boston/Milwaukee Braves. A black cap with a red bill and a white block "M." Great uniform. I raced home to put it on. Brenda was impressed. So was my father, incredibly, who--more incredibly--offered to play catch. But when I kept flinching at the balls he tossed back to me, he muttered in disgust, "You're afraid of the ball." Which I was. And as he walked away, he said over his shoulder, "Maybe Joe Hurley will teach you how to catch a ball." Treasonous child.

When it began to become clear that we would all move on with Joe to a new place and that my father would be going away, I did not regret this new reality. Mary and Patty tell me they remember the day my father left the house--sometime in January or February 1955. I'm not sure if I remember. I carry an image somewhere of a man hauling a suitcase down that big, snow-filled lawn in Burlington. Is it a memory? Too cinematic, I think. In any case, my father left. And we were prepared to move on with Joe Hurley.

LEXINGTON

We moved on very suddenly the first week of March 1955 to the adjacent town of Lexington, a 10-minute drive away from Burlington. We received no warning. And it seemed, we made no preparations. I don't know how we did this; it seemed to happen from one day to the next. This occurred in the middle of the school year when I was in the fifth grade and Mary in the first. I learned on Friday, March 4 that we were moving the next day. I called my best friend, Paul Gurney, whom I had known since the first grade, and told him that I would not see him on Monday because we were moving. He was incredulous and so was I. I wouldn't see him again for seven years.

Actually, there had been preparations. My mother and Joe had been scouting places to buy throughout the autumn of 1954, and I had sometimes been with them as they reconnoitered the terrain. We'd travelled to Winchester and Medford and who knows where else. In the end, they chose Lexington, the upscale suburb just four miles southwest of Burlington. Lexington, the famous site of the first battle of the Revolutionary War in 1775. After seemingly uninhabited Burlington with its 3,000 scattered rustics, Lexington offered an urbane and elegant contrast. And it was full of people: more than 17,000 lived there in the 1950s. It had a library and a movie theater and a public swimming pool and barber shops (Burlington had none!) and five elementary schools with a sixth under construction.

We moved into an enormous three-story, white-frame house at 2173 Massachusetts Ave. on the corner of Cedar Street at the crest of what was called Concord Hill, so-named because the road led on to neighboring Concord--site of the second battle in the Revolutionary War, of course. All the floors were heated, a welcome step up from Burlington. We occupied the first two floors; eventually we'd rent the third floor to other people. The house was spacious, old-fashioned and creaky with a marvelous front-hall stairway. Plenty of room: Mary and Patty in one bedroom, Ann and Brenda in another (though Ann, in fact, continued to live with Paul and Lorraine Sheeran and their children in Woburn and to attend Burlington High School through her senior year), Joe and my mother in another, and I in my own room. We all shared one bath, not unusual in those prehistoric days.

On the top of the house, there protruded a small windowed turret from which you could see all the way to Lexington Center, nearly a mile distant.

Mary and I immediately started attending the Hancock School, a forbidding Romanesque horror. I was intimidated at first by the other kids who seemed sophisticated and smart and capable. Their spelling and math were better than mine. They knew how to draw nearly invisible margins with their fingernails and rulers on their writing papers; I bit my nails and I couldn't do it. There were other strange rituals here. Kids went home at noon to have their lunches with their mothers. Milk and graham crackers were served for mid-morning snacks. Kids bought savings stamps and kept them in booklets. I had no money to buy savings stamps. But Mary and I endured. We walked to school together, the first time I hadn't taken a school bus. We told everyone we lived with our mother and our uncle--"Uncle Joe"--who was our mother's brother. This was plausible, we supposed.

My mother and Joe seemed happy at first in Lexington. Over time, issues developed and fissures appeared. My mother grew suspicious of rivals. She suspected him, with reason, of seeing other women. She began to drink in secret. Things became erratic and volatile and byzantine. This unfolded slowly over a matter of years.

I said that I liked Joe Hurley. The truth was more complicated. I was impressed by him, and intimidated by him and wary of him. I wanted him to like me and to admire me but was unsure how to accomplish this. We shared some tastes. We both enjoyed watching boxing matches on TV. We liked old movies. We both loved the Marx Brothers; my mother did not like them at all--she said they were "rude." I believe Joe thought my mother had failed to discipline me adequately and had indulged my tendency to talk too much. I think he found me a know-it-all. He declared that I was "obnoxious," and when one of my sisters reported this to me and I turned to my mother for an explanation, she dismissed it as a mere joke, an ironic term of endearment for a precocious child. But what it actually meant, I suspect, was that Joe Hurley found me to be obnoxious.

Now that he was no longer a priest, Joe had to find some other way of making a living. He became an entrepreneur. Which is to say, he bought and sold things--mostly cars--but other stuff as well--furniture, clothing, cleaning supplies, tools, whatever--which he found advertised for sale in newspapers and which he'd purchase and resell. He bought houses and then sold them. He bought a car wash. For a while, he operated a realty company--Queensland Realty. Then he purchased a nursing home in neighboring Woburn, and my mother and Ann worked there--Ann in one harrowing episode having to masquerade as a nurse.

Uncle Joe and my mother used to like to take us for long rides in the country on Sundays. Joe always had beautiful cars, usually just two or three years old; these were the ones he was preparing to sell. We'd have Cadillacs and Lincolns and Imperials pulled up on the lawn of the house, doubtless to the annoyance of the neighbors. We'd drive to Concord or Lincoln or Acton and stop for ice cream or at a fruit stand and buy vegetables or cider. I'd want to keep track of the different makes of cars we'd encounter on the trip, so I'd get a block of paper and write down on the left margin the names of all the cars that existed--Ford, Mercury, Lincoln, Chevrolet, Pontiac, etc.--and as we drove along, I'd put a check beside each model we'd pass or see. I knew each one by sight. At the end of the drive, I'd pass on my report to my mother, Joe, Mary and Patty so that they could know precisely how many Plymouths and DeSotos they'd seen that day.

For the first time in my life I lived in a neighborhood teeming with boys my age. All along Cedar Street, which bordered our house on the west, there were kids like me: Robby Weeks and Billy Lofton and Peter Fletcher and Barry St. George and Steve Johnson and Charlie and Johnny Bentley and others whose names I've forgotten. I was out constantly with them doing one thing or another: rolling marbles in the dirt in a kind of crude miniature golf; building small tar-paper shacks and lighting them on fire; participating in furious snow ball fights featuring mass attacks on enormous, meticulously-constructed snow forts; rollicking through the extensive woods behind Peter Fletcher's house in a game of "guns" in which, if you were "killed"--that is "shot" by someone from the other team--you had to remain "dead" until another member of your own team touched you physically, thereby resurrecting you and propelling you back into the fray. And a high point of our merry company's adventures: the discovery one afternoon of the tattered fragments of a "dirty magazine" featuring a photo layout of "Lucky Pierre" in which we see our Parisian hero lounging in his artist studio surrounded by nude buxom models. What unimagined delights may yet await!

All these kids on Cedar Street became my friends. Except for Jackie Curra. He was a really mean kid. One warm summer night as I was leaving Peter Fletcher's house, Jackie Curra jumped me from the bushes in front of the house and started to beat me up. Totally unprovoked. I'd never been in a fight in my life. I was astonished and frightened and then furious. Somehow I got my arms around Jackie's head and got some kind of a headlock on him and began squeezing with all my might even as he was punching me. And then he stopped punching and said he couldn't breathe and begged me to release him. I had won. He walked off quickly and didn't bother me again. I still don't know how I did that.

Peter Fletcher was a good athlete, an especially good baseball player. We'd play catch and he saw that I was hopeless. But he took me with him for Little League tryouts in spring 1955. He was immediately chosen for a major league team, the Tigers--the teams in Lexington were named after major league baseball teams. I didn't make the majors, of course. Discouraged, I soon quit. I turned my energies to swimming. Lexington had a large, professionally-staffed public swimming pool a short bike ride from our house. Starting in the summer of 1955 and for the next three summers, I was there every day when the sun was shining. I became a good swimmer and progressed through the kids' rankings until by 1957 I had become a "Salmon" and could navigate four lengths of the Olympic-sized pool doing the Australian crawl without stopping.

In the fall of 1955 a new elementary school--the Maria Hastings School-- opened, and this was the school Mary and I attended, joined now by Patty in the first grade. I was in the sixth grade. I had a wonderful teacher, Mrs. Geaghan. She was intelligent, creative, kind and beautiful. She recognized special talents in our class and mobilized us to present a musical which she had conceived some years before but which, until we came along, she had not found a group with the chops to bring off. She thought we could do it. And we did! In spring 1956 we presented "A Modern Aladdin" to a full house in the school auditorium one Friday evening. I sang "Be Kind to Your Parents" as a member of a trio. That class was filled with interesting, engaging kids, a number of whom would become my friends and companions through junior high and high school: Jean McMahon, Janice Murray, Jimmy Saulnier, Tommy Napoli, John Thoren, Nancy MacDonald--who, because her last name was identical to mine--would invariably be confused as a relative and be seated next to me in class, and later in homeroom in high school. Nancy and I eventually yielded to the gag and would introduce each other as "cousins."

My sixth grade teacher, Mrs. Geaghan. Spring 1956.

MODEL CARS AND SHIPS

When I was seven or eight years-old, in 1952 or 1953, I began to build plastic model cars and planes and ships. I became good at it.

I started with antique model cars from the early 20th century. Stutz Bearcats and Stanley Steamers and Model Ts. Then sleek Jaguars and postwar British racing cars and MGs. The Revell Company produced beautifully detailed kits of all these cars. You had to paint the pieces first using tiny brushes and miniature bottles of enamel. Once the paint had dried, there might be decals to apply--which could be a delicate and tricky operation--and then you assembled the pieces using epoxy glue.

I moved on from automobiles to warships (U.S. Navy, World War II vintage, of course). The Fletcher-class destroyer "The Sullivans;" the heavy cruiser "Boston;" best of all, the battleship "Missouri" in dazzling black, gray, and off-white camouflage. And from warships, on to Second World War aircraft. The B-17 "Flying Fortress;" the Messerschmitt ME-109; the predatory, gull-winged Stuka dive bomber, the Junkers JU-87.

Smith's Paper Store, on Mass. Ave. in Lexington Center sold model kits and all the paints and brushes and glue and the rest of the apparatus that went with these things. Each year, Smith's sponsored a model building contest as a promotion for their products. The completed entries were displayed in their big front window. I won first place every year I entered for three consecutive years--1956, 1957 and 1958. Then I stopped building models.

JUNIOR HIGH SCHOOL

After the comfortable nest of Mrs. Geaghan's sixth grade at the newly-opened Maria Hastings School, I was tossed with my classmates in the fall of 1956 into the frenzy of junior high school where kids from all six elementary schools in Lexington were scrambled into a newly integrated whole. We were arranged into classes, hierarchically by someone's assessment of our academic abilities and moved as units from homerooms with one teacher and subject matter to other rooms with different teachers and different subjects. I found myself in class 7D, reputed to be one of the brighter seventh grade classes.

This was an unfamiliar, unpleasant place. I knew only, I think, four kids in 7D from the sixth grade: Jean McMahon, Janice Murray, Nancy MacDonald, and Richard Wenzelberger. The other 25 or so students in the class were strangers. I was intimidated by their brightness. I was even more put off by their wealth and social confidence, by the subtle and not-so-subtle class differences that separated them from me. These were kids with professional parents, kids whose fathers were doctors and lawyers and college professors, whose fathers owned real estate companies, whose mothers did not work and who drove them to school in sleek station wagons when it was raining. These were kids who actually had passports and who went skiing, for God's sake.

I was restive among these classmates at first. I longed for a more heterogeneous place. I wanted to be among kids I felt to be more like myself--slightly rougher hewn, not as wealthy, maybe not as smooth, not as ambitious. I broached, obliquely, the subject of transferring to another class. My mother would not hear of my slipping from the pinnacle of 7D downward to one of the lower orders. I would stay put.

There was another thing that had me concerned as I began the seventh grade that fall: I was apprehensive about the prospect of taking the required shower with the other boys after gym class. As an only boy, I had never showered or bathed with another child. I was very self-conscious about my body. I was younger than just about everyone in my class, having started school when I was only five, and I was small for my age, so I was embarrassed at my size and my lack of physical development. I was afraid I'd appear childlike when I undressed for the gang showers. I was afraid I'd be laughed at.

So on the occasion of that first shower, I dawdled initially at the locker I shared with a classmate, Charlie Leto. Only at the last moment, as the other naked boys poured past into the shower room, howling and jostling, did I finally throw off my clothes and run in to join them. No one laughed or even noticed me. I was one of the boys! It was wonderful and liberating! I was completely happy.

We moved as a group from classroom to classroom, from teacher to teacher, from subject to subject: science, social studies, math, English, library science, art, music appreciation, shop (for boys), home economics (for girls), gym (a lot of dancing with the girls, especially the foxtrot). Our homeroom teacher, Mrs. Houghton, was also our English teacher. She was a wonderful instructor who loved literature and taught us that it was important to speak and write clearly and carefully. We read "The Yearling" by Marjorie Kinnan Rawlings with her, and although I initially resisted the book for some reason, the ending touched me deeply. When, at the conclusion of the novel, young Jody goes back and finds that his flutter-mill has been irretrievably broken by the flood, I was moved to tears. Mrs. Houghton read "Charlotte's Web" out loud to us as a class, and we were charmed and smitten that this formidable woman would be so enchanted by this lovely story that she would want to read it to us as if we were, in some way, her children.

By the conclusion of the seventh grade, my initial alienation from my classmates in 7D had evaporated. I'd grown to like them; we were friends. When school began in September 1957 after summer vacation, I was relieved and pleased to find myself reunited with the same cohort of kids, now all eighth graders, in a class designated 8G.

The summer of 1957 had been spent mostly at our newly-built cottage on Niles Beach in Gloucester except for one notable weekend in early August when I stayed home alone in Lexington in order to take the swimming test to qualify as a "Salmon" at the public pool. I took and passed the test on Friday, August 9. The next day I engaged in some memorable and farcical mischief. After participating in the free swim that Saturday morning, I and five or six other boys somehow sneaked back into the pool after it had closed for the weekend. We were cavorting around loudly in the water, splashing off the diving board and raising hell, when we saw a police car pull up across the adjacent field; one of the neighbors must have called the cops. As the police were making their leisurely way towards the pool, we sprang from the water, threw on our clothes over our wet bathing suits, propped seating planks from bleachers against the fences that ringed the pool and scurried up the planks and out. My friend, Larry Spidle, grabbed my bike which I'd hidden in some shrubs, I jumped on the handle bars--Larry was big and I was small--and Larry pedaled us furiously away down the lane behind Parker Street. I jumped off at Mass. Ave., Larry headed off toward his house on my bike, and I ran all the way home up Concord Hill expecting to be intercepted and arrested by the police at any second. I was not.

Thus I eluded incarceration and was able to begin the eighth grade as scheduled one month later.

The eighth grade, the second and last year of junior high school in Lexington in those years, was just about the best year I ever enjoyed in school in terms of grades. I think I got an A in almost every subject in almost every term, even in math where I was weakest and which I liked the least. I can't explain this success except that I think I was buoyed by that cohesive group of kids in 8G and I know that we had a cadre of terrific teachers that year: Mr. Molloy in social studies, Mr. Nickerson in math (also our homeroom teacher), Mr. Terry in science, Mrs. Holmes in English (she looked like Doris Day). Everything fell into place that year. In the spring of 1958, the entire school put on an enormous vaudeville show under the direction of Mr. Molloy, a real showman. The kids sang songs ("Sippin' Sodas," "I Only Have Eyes For You") and performed comedy skits and dance routines. I was a prop man and helped with scenery which is exactly what I wanted to do.

In the course of the eighth grade I encountered a book that would focus and refine my interest in the history of the Second World War: H.R Trevor-Roper's "The Last Days of Hitler." This is a splendid book with an interesting history of its own. Shortly after the conclusion of the war in Europe in 1945, Stalin--who knew perfectly well that Hitler had committed suicide in his bunker beneath the chancellery in Berlin--had his intelligence services circulate stories that Hitler had somehow slunk away to Argentina or Portugal or Spain or that the British were offering him sanctuary in their occupied zone in Germany where they were plotting anti-Soviet designs with the unrepentant Fuehrer. The British, anxious to put an end to these rumors, recruited one of their own intelligence officers, Hugh Trevor-Roper, who was in civilian life a historian of medieval Europe at Oxford, to investigate the circumstance of Hitler's death. Trevor-Roper spent two years on the case, interviewing all the witnesses he could find--the ones who were not in Russian captivity--who had been with Hitler in the bunker in the final weeks of his life. The result of this detective work was published in 1947 as "The Last Days of Hitler."

I read the book 10 years later, and I was mesmerized. It was a masterpiece: a brilliant analysis of a charismatic leader in decline surrounded by a bizarre, dysfunctional court, and it was also a meticulous reconstruction of the events in the Berlin bunker during the second half of April 1945. The language was magisterial and orotund. These are its opening sentences:

Now that the New Order is past and the Thousand Year Reich has crumbled in a decade, we are able at last, picking among the still smoking rubble, to discover the truth about this fantastic and tragical episode. It is a chastening as well as an interesting study; for we discover not only the true facts but the extent of our own errors.

I loved this language. Its confidence and rhythm. And the words: "tragical," "chastening." I wanted to be able to write like this.

Other things happened that year. Sometime during the spring of 1958 we got a dog, a black Labrador Retriever whom we named Smokey. He was a solid, strong, mid-sized creature--intelligent and affectionate. We had always had cats around the house and had never paid them very much attention, but we embraced Smokey as a beloved pet. When the dog was about six months old, one of the young Air Force officers who worked at Hanscom with my mother volunteered to teach him to hunt. I went along on these early Saturday morning training sessions as we put the dog through his paces and he learned to follow commands and to fetch decoys from brush and from ponds and to return them undamaged in his big, soft mouth. Smokey was in ecstasy. I never went on the actual hunts, but by all accounts, he performed magnificently. He roamed free outdoors in Lexington at first; it was something of a miracle he wasn't killed by a car on busy Mass. Ave. But later, after the introduction of leash laws, it became impossible to take care of him because there was no one home during the day to walk him. Eventually--I think during the time I was in the Army, when Smokey was about six years old--my mother had to find another home for him and send him away. She loved the dog, and this was a hard thing for her to do.

LOOKING BACK AT 1958

We were a homogenous bunch, those Lexington Junior High School kids in 1958. Despite my genuinely-felt early perceptions of the economic and social differences that separated me from my classmates, the truth was that we were substantially all middle class and that the differences among us in wealth were slight in the grand scale of things. And there were virtually no racial divides among us: we were practically all white. There were two, maybe three, black kids in our class of almost 350; one of them, the elegant Doreen Hazel, was in my homeroom. I don't believe there were any Asians or Latinos.

This white student universe was dominated by a large block of kids of Anglo-Irish heritage which constituted not quite a majority of the class. I count 164 English, Irish, and Scotch-Irish surnames among the 344 students (48%) who would graduate from Lexington High School in 1962. Names like Allen and Aldrich, Burns and Callahan, Potter and Sullivan and MacFarlane and King and Murphy. The remaining students, the rest of the class whose ancestors did not originate at some point from the British Isles, constituted a rich admixture of kids with Italian names (Balduzzi, Carpenito, Ferrari, Cavaretta), French names (Beaupre, Beauchesne, Boisvert, Marsan), Scandinavian names (Bergin, Kirsten, Thorsen, Lindquist), German-Jewish names (Golden, Goldberg, Wexler, Weiner), Middle-Eastern names (Adzigian, Anastasy, Zagzoug), German names (Schulte, Maurer, Ludwig), Eastern European names (Nawoichik, Oley, Uraneck).

We wore our ethnic differences lightly, bouyed by the natural, self-evident privilege of our whiteness. We got along well. We were pretty innocent. There was routine ethnic banter back and forth, but it was usually benign except for an occasional sputter of unreflective, adolescent antisemitism.

We were not rebellious. The times did not encourage rebellion--that would come later, but not in the 1950s. The decade has a bad reputation, of course. It was, we are told, a period of social and political and cultural conformity, a bland and boring moment in American history when people passively accepted prescribed roles and norms and never challenged the authority--whether formal or informal, governmental or ecclesiastical or aesthetic or educational--that issued such prescriptions. So, yes, we were obedient children; we were "good kids." But we were not inert; we were not stupid. We were intrigued by that sneer of James Dean; we liked that curl in the middle of Bill Haley's forehead; we noticed that Little Richard was wearing eyeliner; we were impressed by the impudence of Marlon Brando in "The Wild Ones" when the girl asks him, "Hey, Johnny, what are you rebelling at?" and he replies, "Whadda got?"

AN ALTAR BOY

It had long been understood that I would become an altar boy when I turned 12 in 1957. I anticipated this with no pleasure. But resistance would have been futile--suicidal, even.

So, sometime in the winter of 1956-57, my instruction began. Every Friday afternoon, I and seven or eight other boys under similar sentence met in a small office in the basement of old St Brigid's Church--scheduled for demolition and replacement by the new St. Brigid's already being built next door. Our teacher was Father MacLeod, young and approachable. A good teacher who connected with us, assuaged our anxieties and set forth clearly what we had to learn.

Which was, that we had to memorize and repeat verbatim a series of responses and prayers in Latin (totaling about 330 words), the sequence of which must never vary, and to master the choreography of a meticulous public dance and performance, again, the sequence of which must never vary, and which would take between 45 and 60 minutes depending upon how many people attended Mass how long the priest decided to talk during his sermon. We would be trained to engage in a public dialogue with the priest, a ritualized back and forth, in which we would substitute for the public who watched, mostly in silence, from the pews beyond the altar. My first words at Mass were always *Ad Deum qui laetificat juventutem meam,"* and I would always conclude, appropriately, with *"Deo gratias."*

None of this was particularly difficult or intellectually challenging. There was some satisfaction in executing these drills, in memorizing these rote tasks. It was gratifying, on one level, to be able to rattle off the Latin, even if you had no idea what you were saying. I was more than a year away from the classical Latin I would encounter in high school--the Latin of Caesar and Cicero and Virgil. (The first sentences in that ninth grade Latin primer were *"Sicilia est insula. Italia non est insula."* There are truths one does not forget.) If I didn't understand what I was saying as an altar boy, no one else--except perhaps the priest--understood what was being said during Mass either. This was standard Roman Catholic procedure in 1957.

In spring 1957 I successfully completed my training and joined the ranks of the altar boys in St. Brigid's parish. I served my first Mass in the old church shortly before it was demolished. I normally served one Mass each Sunday and then there were Holy Days of Obligation and occasional funerals and weddings. I rarely served funerals or weddings and remember little about them.

*Around the time I became an altar boy, April 1957. The tower of
old St. Brigid's Church looms in the background.*

Mass preparations ran smoothly. You came early, picked up cruets of wine and water at the rectory and brought them to the sacristy adjacent to the altar. You chose a black cassock and a white surplus from among those hanging behind the altar. I always looked for a plain, undecorated surplus. The frilly ones looked like doilies and seemed unmanly to me; I was afraid I'd look like a sissy. Then you'd light the candles on the altar and arrange the cruets on the small table on the altar from whence they would be retrieved and brought to the priest and poured into his chalice as part of the communion ceremony. You made sure the bells were positioned correctly.

Some priests allowed us to use prayer cards--texts of the Latin Mass that you placed before you as you knelt to assist with the recitation of what you had memorized. At St. Brigid's, Monsignor Casey, Father MacLeod, and Father Fitzpatrick were all reasonable souls who raised no objections to the use of these cheat sheets. Not so Father Hogan (yet another Irishman). Hogan was a prick and would not allow the use of the cards. We all hated him.

I served as an altar boy for about a year, into the early summer of 1958. I didn't resign or do anything dramatic and quit. I guess I just stopped volunteering and they stopped calling. Once, when accompanying my mother to Mass at Hanscom Air Base where she served as organist at the base chapel, the airman scheduled to serve as altar boy failed to show up and the chaplain-- informed I was an altar boy--asked me to step in. Which I did. And my mother was enormously pleased.

I made friends with some of the kids I served Mass with. Charlie Piggott was the best. He was the quintessential hot shit: a brazen, profane wiseguy. He would go on to become a Marine pilot and would die in a mid-air accident over Vietnam in 1967. Charlie and I shared a deep skepticism about Catholic doctrine and the claims and pretensions of the Church. He thought everything we were doing on the altar was preposterous. One time, when the Mass had ended and we were cleaning up in the sacristy, he chugged down the unconsumed sacramental wine when the priest was in the bathroom.

Since Charlie and I were in the same grade in junior high school, we also found ourselves in the same Sunday School class that met immediately after Mass in the church rectory. The instructor was an earnest layman, unprepared for a restive, insolent bunch of smartass 13-year-olds. One Sunday, the instructor was describing the wonders of the sacrament of penance, how, if one received the sacrament at the moment of death, all one's sins would be forgiven and one would be guaranteed salvation and immediate entry into heaven. Warming to his subject, our instructor related how in the old days, European monarchs had kept a court priest close at hand at all times so that should the prince suddenly be struck down by a fatal illness, he might be administered the soul-saving miraculous sacrament at the last moment and his life of criminal trespass could be redeemed.

At this, Charlie pounced and the dialogue before our rapt group proceeded somewhat as follows:

Charlie Piggott: "So, if Hitler, let's say, had confessed his sins just before he died and the priest had granted him forgiveness and performed the sacrament of penance, he would have gone to heaven?"

Instructor: "Hitler was not a very good Catholic."

C.P.: "That's why he needed to confess and receive penance."

Instructor: "I don't believe Hitler kept a priest in his entourage."

C.P.: "I don't believe he did either. But if he had."

Instructor: "Well, then, yes. The priest could have forgiven his sins."

C.P.: "And all his sins would have been forgiven?"

Instructor: "Technically, yes."

C.P.: "Technically? Killing six million Jews?"

Instructor: "Technically."

C.P.: "And he would have gone to heaven?"

Instructor: "[Triumphant!] No. Because then Hitler killed himself, didn't he? Suicide is a mortal sin. Once he was dead, Hitler could not confess this sin and it could not have been forgiven. He would have died in a state of sin and he would have gone to Hell!"

C.P.: "So let me get this straight. God lets Hitler off the hook for killing six million Jews. But then God sends Hitler to Hell for killing Hitler?"

Instructor: "Technically."

RAY MCGUIGGIN

In the fall of 1956, when she was a sophomore at Boston College, Ann started going out with Ray McGuiggin. I liked him at once. He was tall and blond with a crew cut and thick, horned-rim glasses. He looked like Bill Cullen, the then ubiquitous TV game-show host and panelist.

Ann and Ray off on a date. Lexington. Spring 1959.

Ray was affable and talkative and gregarious. He could tell a million stories about television shows and public personalities and politicians. He made you laugh. Mary and Patty loved him. He always brought them ice cream sundaes and frappes from Brighams when he came to the house to pick up Ann for a date. He was a movie fan and possessed an encyclopedic knowledge of the great films from Hollywood's golden era of the 30s and 40s. Ray was an Irishman from Boston who lived and died by the Red Sox; he had endured all their agonies. Under his influence, my interest in baseball revived. He and I watched games together on TV; he taught me how to keep score. He took me to a game at Fenway Park in 1959 when the team was terrible and the place was half empty, and I understood on that occasion for the first time that I was seeing Ted Williams in person (he was only pinch-hitting--in this, his one season when, because of an injury, he did not hit .300) and he popped-up on the first pitch.

Joe Hurley didn't like Ray. I think he suspected, correctly, that Ray detected him to be a fraud. He was cool toward Ray and endeavored to turn my mother against him.

Ray had served two years in the Army before going to Boston College where he and Ann met. He was one year behind her at BC but older than she because of his time in the Army. I couldn't know it when I first met him, but his career path would become a model for me when I finished high school.

GLOUCESTER

One Friday night during our first summer in Lexington--probably in July 1955--my mother came home from work at Hanscom Air Base and announced that we had to escape from the unbearable heatwave that had descended on us by going to the beach for the weekend. We had no air conditioning in those days, of course. But there was also no nearby Revere Beach anymore. And the family crisis precipitated by my mother's taking up with an ex-priest meant we could no longer seek refuge in her aunt's seaside house in Marblehead. But off we went, my mother and Joe and Mary and Patty and I, without preparations, in the general direction of the Atlantic Ocean.

We didn't find a place to stay until we had driven north for more than six hours on old Route 1. We ended up, the five of us, packed into a rundown, rickety guesthouse--a real dump--blocks from the ocean in Old Orchard Beach, Maine. At least we were on the ocean.

Old Orchard Beach, Maine. Summer 1955.

This experience convinced my mother that we had to get our own weekend getaway by the sea. Somehow she managed to persuade Joe to go along with this scheme, and over the next year and a half, they began to scout out possible sites. They avoided the popular and expensive (and more distant) Cape Cod and instead looked to the "North Shore" to Cape Ann and finally settled on the gritty, working-class fishing town of Gloucester. By the spring of 1957 we had acquired a sliver of property on Eastern Point, directly across the street from Niles Beach in Gloucester Harbor. On this property we built a modest, one-room, wood-framed cottage that sat on a rock escarpment perched over the street and the beach. The cottage's large windows afforded expansive views of the ocean and the point, which swung around to the east with its great mansions and the distant Dog Bar Breakwater at the entrance to Gloucester Harbor. My mother named the cottage Marguerita after herself.

The Marguerita. August 1957

We spent much of the summer of 1957 and nearly all of the summer of 1958 in that cottage. Those were brilliant summers: the ocean and the beach and the sky beckoned from across the street. I don't recall that it ever rained. Those two summers, when I was 12 and 13 years old were, I think, the happiest of my childhood.

That happiness stemmed not only from the stunning natural beauty of the place, but from the fact that those of us who idled in the Marguerita--Patty and Mary and I, sometimes joined by one of the Sheeran kids or one of Patty's and Mary's friends--flourished under the benign and enlightened regime of Ann, whom my mother had charged with our care. Ann could take on this burden because she herself was enjoying summer breaks from her studies at BC and from her care of the three Sheeran children with whom she'd been living since 1954. She was only 20 years old herself in 1957. But she seemed so grown-up to us. And she was wonderful! Fun to be with, witty, reasonable, rational, kind, quick to laugh, attentive to our needs. No melodrama, no hysteria, no dark suspicions, no conspiracies. These phenomena appeared predictably on the weekends when my mother and Joe showed up from Lexington. We all held our collective breaths for 48 hours until they returned home and our idyll and sanctuary could resume.

Mary and Niles Beach. August 1957.

Niles Beach across the street was a 300-yard-long gently curving swath of grey sand and pebbles delineated by a 10-foot-high stone seawall. Its western terminus, kitty-corner from our cottage, was formed by a massive igneous rock formation on which stood several large turn-of-the-century summer houses. The beach swung around broadly to the east where it ended in a series of low, pink granite terraces that interrupted the sand and slid at intervals into the ocean. Because Niles was located inside Gloucester Harbor and was therefore protected by its breakwater, one rarely encountered any noteworthy waves. Niles was a "family beach," a safe place for little kids. It offered no amenities. There were no bath-houses, no toilets; you couldn't get a pizza or an ice cream there. It was a beach for locals, for people from the neighborhood who walked home for lunch. I spent every day there.

Views of the interior of the cottage in Gloucester at Niles Beach. August 1957.

Most of the time I went snorkeling with two boys, brothers, who lived next door to our cottage and were a couple of years younger than I. They were the sons of the chauffeur who every summer drove a wealthy widow from New Jersey up to Gloucester where she maintained a mansion by the sea. These boys and I went snorkeling in shallow coves just off the beach--the water was 5-8 feet deep--where we hunted and killed crabs for sport. We impaled them with spears fashioned from garden tools. We'd swim across the surface with our faces in the water--masks on and breathing through our snorkels--until we spotted a crab scurrying across the ocean floor and then we'd hold our breaths, dive down, and murder the poor creatures. Wanton boys.

The water was clear and very cold. We wore tee-shirts under the delusion that they would provide some measure of warmth against the icy ocean. After 10 or 12 minutes in the water, we'd come out shivering and unable to breathe. We possessed no body fat. We'd lie on the rocks which on sunny days were baked hot.

I learned the texture and the colors of the beach and the ocean. I came to see that in the shallows the water was a glimmering aquamarine against the yellow sand--a marvelous, soft subtropical presentation that one did not expect in this northern sea. And I learned to watch and understand the enormous sky. You had to know what the sun was going to do if you were going to snorkel: you didn't want to be underwater when the sun was obscured by a cloud. So I learned to read clouds--their direction and speed and opacity.

When I wasn't snorkeling, I built elaborate mud fortresses adorned with intricate structures and then I'd observe them as they were enveloped by incoming tides. I became adept at using the grey-black tidal muck as a quick-drying stucco with which I could create spindly towers and fragile buttresses by letting the mud drizzle carefully from my cupped hands. Having created these miniature temples and cathedrals, I never tired of watching their intimate, minute disintegration as the rising tide--sometimes on quiet Niles Beach, rising imperceptibly with hardly a ripple--nibbled them into nothingness.

When, at the end of the day, we returned to the cottage from the beach, we'd watch TV with Ann. Dick Clark's "American Bandstand" was required viewing. We'd see all the cool teens dancing in Philadelphia and watch the guest pop stars lip-synching their latest hits. Then casual dinners--BLTs or cheeseburgers on the charcoal grill outside. Then reading or checkers or even chess, maybe more TV until the Late Show, one of those Hollywood movies the studios has just released to television. It was then, in the summers of '57 and '58, that I first began seeing all those Errol Flynn movies: "The Dawn Patrol" and "The Charge of the Light Brigade" and "The Adventures of Don Juan." And Flynn would be dead in two years.

One night Ray showed up at the cottage with a special treat. His older brother worked at one of the Boston TV stations where he was responsible for, among other things, broadcasting televised movies. In those days, you simply set up the full projection of the 35 mm. film in the TV studio--just like you were showing it in a theatre--and you merely televised the image. Ray brought up to Gloucester three huge cannisters of 35 mm film, the enormous projector to actually run this stuff, and a portable screen, on which to show it. And there in the Marguerita we watched--in Technicolor!--the 1954 hit movie "Young at Heart" with Doris Day, Frank Sinatra, Dorothy Malone and Gig Young. It was fabulous! It was fabulous even though Ray, in setting up the screen, accidently punched a small hole in one of the ceiling tiles, a calamitous error that would be immediately detected by Joe--and by my mother--and which Joe would interpret--and endeavor to persuade my mother to interpret--as evidence of Ray's recklessness, untrustworthiness, inattention to detail, bad eyesight, negligent personal hygiene, and so on.

The cottage was gone after the summer of 1958. We sold it and bought in its place a large, dreary three-story hotel four blocks from the ocean that had served for a number of years as a vacation site for a Jewish community organization which had moved on to another place. We renamed this horror the Harbor Bell Hotel. It actually consisted of two buildings: the second--tucked away in the rear--was a tall assemblage of miserable, long-neglected apartments. None of the rooms, in either building, afforded a water view. The effort to turn the Harbor Bell into a profitable enterprise was misconceived. Nobody wanted to stay there. (Even though, as an enticement, my mother allowed the infrequent guests the opportunity to select whichever Montovani album they wished to play on the stereo from her extensive selection, which she displayed on large tables next to the dining room.) We departed after only one summer, in 1959.

This was, unfortunately, not the end of my mother's and Joe's careers as hoteliers. In 1961 they bought another hotel on the North Shore, this one in Magnolia. Much of the family--Ann and Ray and Mary and Patty--were drawn into the morass and into the dramas that unfolded there. By taking a job in a supermarket in Lexington, I was spared. Magnolia was not part of my growing up.

Gloucester for me always remained those two magical summers of 1957 and 1958 and that charming little cottage on Niles Beach.

HIGH SCHOOL

I started high school in September 1958 when I entered the ninth grade; I graduated four years later in June 1962. Our class was the last group in Lexington to spend four full years in high school. The Lexington school system reorganized things after we left junior high by building an additional junior high school and by combining the seventh, eighth, and ninth grades together into an expanded junior high and reducing the high school to just three classes--the 10th, 11th, and 12th. My class would consequently spend two of its four years in high school as the youngest class there.

I was an indifferent student over those four years. I rarely studied or kept up with the readings or completed assigned homework. I bluffed and dodged my way through class discussions. I wrote papers while watching TV and submitted them, unrevised, at the last moment. My grades were no more than fair: some As and Bs in English and social studies and civics, Cs and even Ds in math and science. I never made National Honor Society. None of the subjects interested me. Algebra was incomprehensible, chemistry irrelevant, Latin useless and ultimately too difficult; English was occasionally amusing but there was more Shakespeare than necessary; the social sciences courses that I should have loved were taught by bores. All this in a place with marvelous teachers.

The very good and very dutiful eighth grade student became a lousy high school student. I'm not entirely sure why. Puberty? Inchoate rebelliousness? Bad companions? For whatever reasons, I began to affect an insouciant, cynical, smart-guy pose toward things academic--indeed toward most things. Everything was a joke, contemptibly stupid, "a farce"--a favorite word. The truth was, I think, that I was insecure and unsure of my ability to succeed in this new realm amidst some very bright people who were really well-read--who had not invented the books they claimed to have read--and who were prepared to work hard and apply themselves and take the expectations of this new realm seriously. Instead, I chose to mock those expectations and the people who took those expectations seriously. I would become a wit; I would glide through high school armed with a smirk and a joke and a glib tongue. I was prepared to learn nothing--and apart from mastering the mysteries of the stick shift in drivers ed--I largely succeeded.

In my senior yearbook, a friend wrote over her class picture a personal note intended, I'm sure without irony, as high praise: "Dear Steve, I really mean it when I say that I know you will be a great success. You can talk your way into anything, so you've got nothing to worry your own sweet self about." High praise for the gifted debater and extemporaneous orator and for the con man and grifter.

High school unspooled not as an educational experience, but as a series of shifting, sometimes overlapping, oftentimes confusing social arrangements and alliances beginning with a stimulating friendship with Alex Humez that spanned my freshman and sophomore years.

I met Alex in the first days of high school. I had not known him in junior high, but I found him to be very cool: smart and whippet quick and seditious. He was a smallish kid, like me, but exceptionally good looking and attractive to girls some of whom found his 50s tough-guy good looks irresistible. He combed his blond hair into an amazing rocker pompadour that resembled Jerry Lee Lewis's. I was envious. Alex smoked cigarettes--Kent filters--and I started smoking too. There assembled around him a constellation of crude-talking, mischievous characters to whom I gravitated. It pleased me to be welcomed into this company.

I started to swing by Alex's house as I walked to school each morning, and we'd continue on together, smoking cigarettes as we went. After school, we'd hang out with a bunch of boys--no girls--at someone's house and watch TV, tell vulgar jokes, smoke, make random prank phone calls to unwary victims and generally behave stupidly. On Friday nights we often went to the Hayden Recreation Center—"the Rec"--which sponsored sock hops; sometimes Alex and I played the role of DJ and got to pick which 45s were played. We all shared an intense interest in sex. When I visited Alex's house at night to "study" with him (we were in the same English class) we spent most of the time drawing nude women copied from models in Alex's "Learn How to Draw" primer. (My mother would never have permitted me to possess such a thing.) Alex had a copy of "Lady Chatterley's Lover"--maybe it was his father's--and we read and re-read the well-thumbed dirty parts together. Alex, moreover, actually had girlfriends. Which I, despite fumbling efforts, did not.

Alex Humez and I, Lexington Center. Fall 1958.

Every two or three months, whenever we could save up $15 or $20, we would embark on a major expedition into Boston. Alex and I sometimes worked together to get the money we needed by raking leaves in the fall or shoveling snow in winter or by mopping the floors of Joe Hurley's nursing home in Woburn. We were often accompanied on these trips by Alex's friend Dick Slocumbe, an erratic and rather violent personality whom I was actually afraid of. The Boston trips were great adventures. We'd take the local bus from Lexington Center to Arlington Heights, then an MTA bus to Harvard Square, the MTA Red Line subway to Park Street Station in Boston and then we'd walk to Scollay Square, a notoriously squalid and seedy section of the city that would soon be demolished and replaced by Government Center and City Hall. But in those days, it was filled with Dickensian wonders: tiny amusement arcades; overstuffed and nearly inaccessible booksellers; toxic eateries; lurid, salacious entertainments. All that a boy could want.

For starters we'd play some arcade games: pin ball, air hockey, the shooting gallery, duck pins. Then we'd spend hours in labyrinthine, moldering bookstores that offered used paperbacks--the front covers of the books had been cut in half to mark them--and they usually cost only 10 or 15 cents each. You could get a lot of books for a couple of bucks. We were avid readers of science fiction and fantasy. I loved the novels and short stories of Robert Heinlein and Ray Bradbury and Arthur C. Clarke. We'd load up a shopping bag and drag our loot over to Washington Street where we'd share an enormous pizza with root beers at one of the Italian restaurants, and then we'd take in a movie. I remember seeing "Sink the Bismarck" during one of these junkets, and "Al Capone" (with Rod Steiger chewing the scenery as the crazy gangster) and "Journey to the Center of the Earth" (with Pat Boone [!] as co-star). Then back to Lexington via subway and bus and bus. Exhausting and exhilarating.

Alex's mother was a revelation to me. She seemed to me, the outsider, the model of calm, enlightened reason. She was genuinely interested in, and knowledgeable about, what we were studying in school. (This well-educated woman would later teach English at some point in Lexington High School and my sister, Mary, would have her as a teacher.) On one occasion, Alex's mother drove the two of us to Harvard Square to shop at the Harvard Coop. As we were driving back to Lexington, she was expressing her pleasure in the study of Latin which I was then taking--Alex was taking French. I offered to demonstrate my new skills in Latin by saying, "I know how to decline the verb 'amo'." Mrs. Humez looked at me evenly in the rear-view mirror (I was sitting in the back seat), and said: "Stephen, you decline adjectives; you conjugate verbs."

Alex was a talented musician. He could read music and played a number of instruments competently: trumpet, piano, guitar. He decided that we should form a rock group. Joe Hurley owned a Hawaiian guitar, the kind you're supposed to hold flat on your lap and play with a sliding steel bar. But Joe never played it. I seized the thing with the intention of playing it like a normal guitar. But I had no idea how to play it or any other instrument. Alex taught me a few rudimentary chords; I had a passable voice. We teamed with another guitarist and with a kid who owned a decent drum set, and the "Smoke Rings" were born in the winter of 1958-59. Our biggest (and only) hit, played at both our gigs--a junior high dance probably in February 1959 and a dance in the basement of the Church of Our Redeemer, the Episcopal Church, in April--was "Stagger Lee," the cover of a hit song by Lloyd Price.

I was standing on the corner
When I heard my bulldog bark.
He was barking at the two men who were gambling
In the dark.

The brief, incandescent career of the "Smoke Rings" has left no mark on the history of Rock and Roll. I have found no audios, alas, to enrich the photograph presented here. Posterity will never know what we sounded like.

"The Smoke Rings." (L to R): me (in shades), Eddie Winter, Alex Humez.
In the back, obscured, George Sloane on drums. April 1959.

INTERLUDE: PRO FOOTBALL

In the fall of 1958, I and a lot of other people started watching professional football on television for the first time in large numbers. The game had been around for a long time, of course, but it seemed that it really began to attract and hold a mass audience that autumn. This was back when there was only one professional football league--the National Football League--two years before the creation of the upstart American Football League and the founding of, among other new teams, what would first be called the Boston Patriots. What I saw every Sunday afternoon at 1 PM on CBS TV was the New York Football Giants--every game, home and away.

The Giants were great to watch. They were a very successful team which had won the league championship just two years earlier in 1956. Loaded with marquee players like quarterback Charlie Conerly, movie-star-handsome halfback Frank Gifford, wide receiver Kyle Rote, and middle linebacker Sam Huff--whose appearance on the cover of *Time Magazine* in November 1959 would signal mainstream journalism's acknowledgement that professional football had become an entertainment phenomenon. (And, be it noted, still a largely white entertainment phenomenon in those ancient days. The starting 22 players on that 1958 Giants team included only three black men.) I got hooked on this stuff and became a Giants fan even though I knew nothing about football: I didn't even know initially how many yards you had to make to get a first down. Ray McGuiggin was appalled at my enthusiasm for the Giants. His loathing of the Yankees extended to all other New York sports teams, and he regarded my affection for the Giants as little short of treason.

HIGH SCHOOL (CONTINUED)

Sometime during the fall of 1959, early in my sophomore year, my mother decided that I should not continue at Lexington High School. She doubtless noticed my mediocre grades and my undisciplined study habits. She had deduced that I was smoking cigarettes. She concluded that I had fallen in with a bad crowd; she would refer to Alex Humez as "your gangster friend." She had intercepted and opened a letter Alex had written me the previous summer when we were away in Gloucester. I have no idea now what he had written, but I can only imagine that it involved subject matters and language she found objectionable. In any case, my mother determined that I should study under the rigorous tutelage of Jesuit instructors at Boston College High School from which, not coincidentally, Ray McGuiggin had graduated.

I was trundled off one afternoon for a preliminary interview to BC High located then in Alston, across the Charles River from Cambridge. I effectively torpedoed this scheme by my sullen, rude behavior during the interview with the priest in which I responded with a monosyllabic "Yes" and "No" to every question but refused to add the required "Father," despite repeated admonitions to do so. It was obvious to the priest that I didn't want to go to BC High. And so the thing collapsed. My mother was furious at my awful behavior. But it was an ill-conceived idea. How would I have gotten to Alston every day? How would we have paid for a private school? And why would I have transferred from one the best high schools in Massachusetts to begin with? It was a measure of my mother's anxiety about my future that she would have concocted such a plan to begin with. But I would remain in Lexington High School.

In the course of our sophomore year Alex Humez and I drifted apart. We had different interests and ambitions. Alex wanted to perform musically and to take part in school theatre. I was no musician, and the theatre did not attract me. I was drawn to team sports; he was not. He later described himself as being "allergic to pom-poms." My interest in football having been sparked by watching the Giants on TV, I worked the fall 1960 season as one of three "managers"--that is, equipment boys--for the Lexington High football team. Great fun. I'd spend every afternoon with the team and then virtually all day Saturday preparing for the game and then at the game itself. (The team was terrible: no wins, eight losses, one tie. We lost by a cumulative score of 222 to 41!) In the spring of 1961, as a junior, I tried out for the baseball team as a pitcher, my first effort to play organized baseball since I was 10 years old. I didn't make the team: good control, no velocity. A disappointment. But I found myself with old buddies and new friends from these athletic endeavors--guys who often moved in social circles to which I felt drawn. These people, Peter Bergin and Jerry Marsan and Joe Miller and Jimmy Stone and Larry McCarthy and Bobby Sheridan, became good friends during my last two years in high school.

Lexington High School Junior Varsity Football Team, 1960. I'm second from the left, middle row.

We played a lot of pick-up sports together: baseball (and I actually got to pitch in those games), basketball on outdoor courts, hockey (on frozen ponds, and sometimes on ice rented early in the morning at the Boston Skating Club in Cambridge). We went to dances at the high school and to drive-in movies (by this time, plenty of kids had a drivers' license, though I wouldn't get mine until late in my senior year). And we went to lots of Red Sox games. I must have seen 30 games at Fenway Park between 1960 and 1962. The Red Sox were bad in those seasons: they finished seventh out of eight teams in 1960, sixth out of ten in 1961, eighth out of ten in 1962. Did I notice or care that they were owned and managed by indolent racists? They were nonetheless fun to watch because they offered intriguing personalities even if the team played lousy ball. Ted Williams was in his last year in 1960, and I got to see him hit a homerun against the Indians one Sunday in July. Pete Runnels won the American League batting title and played on the same team. Carl Yastrzemski joined the club the next year. The third baseman, Frank Malzone, was the best infielder in the league until Brooks Robinson came up with the Orioles. And in those years, the Red Sox played regular single-admission double-headers on Sundays: two games for the price of one--reserved grandstand cost only $2.50. The park opened at noon; first game at 1 o'clock, second game wouldn't get over until 7 o'clock or 8 o'clock at night. You could sit in Fenway Park all day and watch baseball.

GIRLS

I was very interested in girls in high school but had little success with them. I didn't know how to talk to girls or what to talk about with them. I was shy and self-conscious about my small size. Because I was terribly near-sighted, I started wearing glasses in my freshman year, and I was certain it made me look like a nerd. It seemed impossible to me that a girl would find me attractive. Here's a photograph of me from the 1961 Lexington High School Yearbook, my junior year, taken with other homeroom representatives from my class. I've removed my glasses and I'm straining to appear as tall as I can for the camera. Ridiculous.

Junior Class Homeroom Representatives, Lexington High School, 1961. I'm far left, back row.

It therefore came as an enormous surprise to me sometime around December 1960, when I was 15 and a junior, when a friend confided to me that he had heard a rumor that Tori Porter found me interesting and wanted to go out with me. Tori (for Victoria) Porter was a very attractive sophomore girl who had been actively pursued by some of the fast and aggressive characters at school--the guys with leather jackets and loud cars. I couldn't believe that Tori Porter knew I existed. But somehow she had noticed me. She was very sexy and sweet and we did go out for a few months. She became my first girlfriend. It felt good to have one.

Aside from Tori, I never dated anyone steadily in high school. I had a crush on a girl named Mary Harris whom I took to a Red Sox game and a News Years Eve dance. And Mary and I and a bunch of other kids from Lexington attended Jack Kennedy's election eve rally in Boston Garden the night before Kennedy defeated Nixon in November 1960. I took a classmate, Nancy Coombs, to the junior prom, but I don't think I even attended the senior prom.

There are two noteworthy follow-ups to the Tori Porter story.

The Lee Ballard Story. When Tori and I were going out in 1960-61, we often double-dated with my old friend, Bob Murphy, and with Tori's friend, Lee Ballard. The four of us would get something to eat and then we'd go parking in Bob's enormous Oldsmobile--Bob and Lee in the front seat, Tori and I in the back. The necking was rudimentary and chaste. Five years later, in 1966, when I got out of the Army, I would encounter Lee Ballard again and she and I would become very close, my first real American love affair.

The University of Maine Story. Tori would go on to marry a guy who would get a PhD in biology and take a faculty appointment at the University of Maine at Orono at the same time that I would become a member of the faculty at the University of Maine at Fort Kent and I would move there with my wife in the fall of 1978. Having discovered this coincidence, Tori and I would one night have dinner together in Bangor around 1980--twenty years after our first date in High School-- and smile about our gentle, long-ago encounter as teenagers.

THINGS FALL APART

It had always been assumed that I would go to college after high school. I would become a teacher, probably a history teacher. Perhaps a professor. (My mother might have preferred I become a lawyer, like Uncle Dan and Uncle Frank.) In any case, I would certainly go to college.

We gave little thought to the details. I visited no campuses. I examined no literature comparing schools and conducted no research weighing program options and finances. Ann (and Ray) had graduated from Boston College. And so I applied to BC. I was accepted. I applied nowhere else. I would be a commuter, of course, because we did not have the money for me to be a residential student. The question never entered my mind. We did not consider the logistics of how I would travel the 17 busy miles each day from Lexington to Chestnut Hill and back. We'd figure it out.

During my last two years of high school, as I glided toward an uneventful and undistinguished graduation, our family began to disintegrate.

In the summer of 1960, we moved from the large, three-story house in which we had lived since coming to Lexington in 1955 into a smaller, red-brick house immediately next door. This was a handsome, comfortable place. But it was an unhappy place. Within a year of moving in, Ann and Brenda got into an acrimonious dispute with Joe--and my mother--over the terms of their living there. Something about the use of the telephone and their contributions to family finances. By this time, they were both in their early 20s and were working. I was still a kid and didn't understand any of this. It got nasty and both Ann and Brenda moved out. Ann returned; Brenda did not. When, within a year, Brenda got married, the rest of us did not attend her wedding. I later learned that Brenda called Patty and Mary and offered to pay for their wedding outfits so that they could participate in her ceremony, but my mother would not permit it. Mean Irish stuff. I'm glad I didn't know at the time that this had happened.

In May 1962, Ann and Ray married and went off to establish their own home. (My father was not invited to Ann's wedding--a sign of how deep the gulf had become between him and his children; I walked Ann down the aisle in St. Brigid's that day.) After Ann departed for her new home, Mary and Patty and I were alone with my mother and Joe. Things got bad. My mother had long suspected Joe--with good reason--of chasing other women. Her jealousy and anger had been brewing for years; now the anger became ferocious and violent. She began to drink constantly. Their arguments were terrifying: they began late at night as low, rumbling, spitting protestations and then turned into volcanic, screaming eruptions. Hour after hour into the night and morning. I once fled the house at 1:30 AM and walked down the street to Hastings Green and sat under a stand of trees for 45 minutes to escape the tumult. Mary and Patty would huddle together in fear in their beds. My mother would show me bruises on her arms as evidence of Joe's brutality. Joe would report that he had had to forcibly restrain her from attacking him with knives and pots and pans. This was the summer of 1962, just as I was about to begin my first year of college.

New students reported to Boston College for the fall semester in the middle of September that year. It turned out that I would not be the only kid from the Lexington High School class of '62 attending. Joining me would be Steve Johnson, a long-time friend and neighbor from the Cedar Street gang. It was comforting to go off together to BC with this Lexington High crony--a droll, wise-cracking guy whom I knew from school and St. Brigid's as a fellow altar boy.

We would, in fact, crash and burn within five weeks.

BC offered little in the way of an orientation program for freshman in those days. It was sink or swim. I recall all the new students being jammed into the enormous field house where we got to try to sing the Alma Mater ("For Boston"), were introduced to the football team mascot--a live eagle--and were given a preening lecture about how tough Boston College was, how it was intentionally designed to weed out the unworthy and the unprepared, how we should look at the person sitting to our left and to our right and understand that at least one of these people would not be there at graduation. Or in my case, even by late October. I never met an advisor or discussed my academic program or chose the classes I wished to take. My classes had, in fact, already been chosen for me: rhetoric, logic, Old Testament studies, algebra, chemistry, Latin.

I was appalled. Was I not to be consulted? I intended to be a history major. No history? Math and lab science? Perhaps I should have looked at the graduation requirements. Latin? I had wanted to study a modern language. Old Testament studies? Logic? Apparently this is what you get at a Jesuit institution. And where were the girls? Had I not noticed before now that the only women at BC were enrolled in the Schools of Education and Nursing?

I didn't want to be at this place and I didn't want to take any of these courses.

Moreover, getting to and from BC was awful. At first, Steve and I negotiated the endless series of bus, subway and trolley transfers between Lexington and Chestnut Hill. This took about an hour and a half, one-way, through Arlington, Cambridge, and Boston. The morning commute improved when Steve found a friend of his father's who worked near BC and we were able to catch a ride with him to the college. But we still had to get home. We decided to hitch-hike. Every afternoon after classes, we'd stick our thumbs out on Commonwealth Avenue and try to hitch a ride out to Route 128 where we'd get out and clamber up on the highway and hitch another ride--or rides--the 10 miles or so to Lexington. Depending on our luck, all this could take anywhere from two to three hours. We'd arrive home battered and demoralized. The whole thing was an educational and logistical fiasco.

At this precarious moment, things completely collapsed at home. My mother decided to leave Joe. When I got home from BC on Monday afternoon, Oct. 1, 1962, my mother announced that we were moving that evening from 2161 Mass. Ave.--the red brick house--and going to another house closer to Lexington Center at 1963 Mass. Ave. And so we packed up all our things and piled them in the car and we moved that night about one-half mile down the road into a large, sprawling, three-story place adjacent to the parking lot at St. Brigid's where I had served as an altar boy. We didn't own the whole house; we only rented the first floor and a few rooms on the second floor. Strangers seemed to come and go at will in the place. It was disorienting and unsettling. But the bond with Joe Hurley was broken--or so we thought.

And so it seemed that in the course of a few weeks, the structures and norms and assumptions of my life had fallen away. I was utterly disappointed with and unengaged by Boston College. And my home life--already deeply problematic and riven by my mother's hysteria and melodramas--now appeared to disintegrate in material disarray. BC was awful. Commuting to BC was awful. The new house was awful. I wanted to get away from everything that had become a mess at home and at school. I wanted to get far away from Massachusetts. The lyrics from Henry Mancini's "Moon River," the lead song from "Breakfast at Tiffany's," spoke powerfully to me:

> *Two drifters off to see the world*
> *There's such a lotta world to see.*
> *We're after the same rainbow's end, waitin' round the bend*
> *my Huckleberry friend, Moon River and me.*

It turned out that Steve Johnson wanted to get away too. I thought, at the time, that Steve--unlike me--had a secure home life, but I learned years later that he did not and that he was also looking for an escape. He hated the commute, and hated his academic program and he was no more ready to settle down and study than I was. He discovered a solution: we would join the Army and see the world. On his own initiative he left campus one day and visited the Army recruiting office in downtown Boston and returned with fabulous stories abut how we could join the Army on the "Buddy Plan" that would carry us together through Basic Training and beyond. Steve reported on opportunities available to bright kids like us to learn foreign languages--*modern* foreign languages--in the Army's marvelous Foreign Language Institute in exotic Monterey, California. California! We could get there by joining something called the Army Security Agency, Steve reported--an elite intelligence organization that would spare us the rigors and dangers of infantry squalor. We began fantasizing about "Christmas in Monterey." We even made up a song about it.

I had long entertained romantic notions of military life, nourished by novels and movies about the Second World War and fueled, especially, by the images and the sweeping score from "Victory at Sea." I half imagined that my life was being accompanied by music written by Richard Rogers. Thus I was especially susceptible to the seductive allure of a grandiose escape from the dreary trap that my home life and Boston College had become. I was prepared to leap at the opportunity.

The agreeable fantasy of running off to the Army Language School perched on the cliffs high above the Pacific absorbed and overpowered our imaginations. By the end of October, five weeks or so after starting college, Steve and I pretty much stopped attending classes. (This was, coincidentally, exactly when the Cuban Missile Crisis erupted.) When I told my mother I wanted to leave college and join the Army, she was dismayed. I reminded her that Ray McGuiggin had served in the Army before attending college, and that all had worked out well for him, but she was unconvinced. She urged me to talk to one of her priest friends who urged me to reconsider. I did not. On Nov. 14, 1962, Steve Johnson and I were sworn in as privates in the U.S. Army at the Boston Army Base. I enlisted for three years in the Army Security Agency. Serial number: RA (for Regular Army) 11-412-717.

BASIC TRAINING

First stop: Fort Dix, NJ. This was the Basic Training destination for new inductees from the Northeast and mid-Atlantic. Army Basic Training in those days had none of the cinematic lunacy one associates with Marine boot camp. We were not subjected to the ravings of psychotic, sadistic sociopaths masquerading as drill instructors. Our platoon sargents were laid-back career infantry non-commissioned officers--almost all of them Black--who found in the Army a welcome haven from the racism of contemporary America. They went about the business of accustoming the indolent civilians in their charge to the strange rituals of military life with minimum fuss. At least half of the new soldiers around me were draftees who endured this transformation sullenly and without enthusiasm.

As promised, Steve Johnson and I were assigned to the same unit: Alpha Company, Third Battalion, Fourth Training Regiment. Within that company, people were placed in one of four platoons in alphabetical order: Steve ended up in the Second Platoon, I was in the Third. Each platoon consisted of about 50 men and was housed in a separate two-story wooden barracks that dated from World War II. I didn't see much of Steve. My platoon sergeant, Sgt. Campbell, was a tall, good-looking man who spoke in a deep baritone and intimidated us with his stares and long silences. He had seen combat in Korea. We learned that he was kind and slow to anger.

The Company's First Sergeant, Bernie Riley, was the only white man among the non-coms. He was a witless buffoon, perpetually drunk. He burst into our barracks at 5:30 AM on Tuesday, Dec. 8, 1962 shouting up the stairwell, "Are there any fucking Catholics up there! You get to go to Mass this morning, you bastards! It's a fucking Holy Day, you know!" We staggered from our beds in confusion listening and laughing at this tirade. Riley went on. "You probably think I'm a fucking Catholic because my name is Riley. But I'm not a fucking Catholic! I'm from Northern Ireland! I'm a fucking Protestant!" Those of us who were Catholic took advantage of this opportunity and attended chapel that morning, because it was, in fact, a Holy Day of Obligation: the Feast of the Immaculate Conception. Thank you, Bernie Riley.

We spent most of our time in Basic Training learning how to shoot a rifle in a rigorous sustained exercise called "Train Fire." We were still using the Garand M-1 semi-automatic rifle developed in the 1930s and introduced as the standard American infantry weapon in World War II. This was a tough, sturdy and extremely accurate rifle, and it was fun to learn how to use the thing. I had had a BB gun as a kid, but I think I had only fired a real rifle once before in my life, so it was an adventure to be out on a firing range nearly every day--even in winter--shooting constantly. That rifle was terrific. But you had to be careful loading it. You'd slide the clip with eight 30-calibre bullets into the breech with your thumb while holding the bolt back with the heel of your palm, and once the clip was in place, you lifted your palm quickly letting the bolt slam forward while making sure to get your thumb out of the way or else the bolt would catch your thumb. "M-1 Thumb." Painful.

All this practice concluded in a two-day qualification shooting test. On each day, you are given seven clips--56 bullets--and taken to an outdoor shooting range, a long narrow field, maybe 30 yards wide and about 400 yards deep. The field has light brush and few trees. A firing instructor sits beside you with a scorecard. He signals you to load the rifle. Then he blows a whistle. Suddenly, in front of you, man-sized cardboard targets start to pop up in the field; some of them are 20 yards in front of you, some of them are at 50 yards or 100 yards or 200 yards or 350 yards. Some on the right, some on the left, some in the middle. You don't know where they will appear. They stay up for five seconds; then they disappear. You have five seconds to shoot them. After eight shots your clip is empty. You have to put in another clip. The targets don't slow down. After two clips, the instructor tells you to lie flat and continue shooting. After four clips, he tells you to jump into the foxhole on your left and continue shooting. You see a target pop up 350 yards out. That's three and a half football fields away. Knowing that gravity will pull the bullet downward, I aim above the target. I squeeze the trigger. I hit the thing. I use up all my clips. The instructor says, "Nice shooting."

That evening, I'm dressing after my shower and Sgt. Campbell seeks me out in the barracks. "MAC Donald," he says, and lowers his huge face to mine. Have I done something wrong, I wonder. He smiles. "You shot the SHIT out of that place today," he says. He is holding a score card of the platoon's first-day performance. I hit 43 out of 56 shots, he tells me. Next day, I hit 41 out of 56, and I end up with a combined score of 84 out of 112--fourth best in Alpha Company, best in Campbell's platoon.

Campbell is pleased but disappointed that someone with my gifts as a rifleman remains committed to the plan to attend Language School, to become what the sergeant calls a "Monterey Mary." But that's what Steve Johnson and I are determined to do. First, however, we have to pass the Army Language Aptitude Test. This was administered to a small group of about 30 of us who had all enlisted--like Steve and me--for the Army Security Agency. We took the language test along with a battery of additional exams measuring our suitability for other jobs in the Agency: wireless intercept operator, codebreaker, communications analyst and so on. The language test was designed to assess our capacity to make sense of a new language, our ability to infer meaning from the patterns of syntax and structures and repetition of an artificial language. The examination would presumably indicate our facility in learning a real foreign language.

The language test has 50 questions. The officer administering the test informs us that we need 17 correct answers to pass. We should not guess, he advises us: the number of incorrect answers will be subtracted from the number of correct answers in calculating the score. It is better to leave answers blank, he says. We begin. The test is interesting, and I know at once I am doing well. I am soon sure that I have at least 17 correct answers. I proceed deliberately. Better to leave some questions blank than to rush too fast. Within a few days we have the results: Steve

Johnson has scored 33; I have scored 32. We both have passed. We will soon be off to Monterey! But wait. After a few more days we receive another report: too many people have passed the test, it appears, so the bar must be raised on the scoring. The passing score is not to be 17; it will be 33. Steve Johnson is going to Monterey, California where he will learn Korean. Steve MacDonald is going to Fort Devens, Massachusetts where he will learn to become a communications analyst.

I was mortified. My grand plan to flee Lexington and see the world had, after three months, brought me to the dreary backwater of Ayer, Mass. exactly 23.8 miles from where I had started.

FORT DEVENS

The Army Security Agency (ASA) was the U.S. Army's signals intelligence branch. Its mission was both offensive--to gather military intelligence, strategic and tactical, about foreign armies by penetrating their communications systems--and defensive--to safeguard the Army's communications systems from foreign penetration. The ASA had been created in 1945 at the dawn of the Cold War and lasted as an autonomous Army unit until 1976 when it was consolidated into the Army's Military Intelligence branch. The ASA was not like the rest of the Army. Its people were well-educated: the enlisted ranks had an average of 14 years of schooling. And in an Army that was largely integrated racially, the ASA was overwhelmingly white. In my two and one-half years of service in the ASA, I recall encountering six people of color: two Blacks (one an officer) two Hispanics (one an officer) and two Asians. This didn't happen by accident. Recruiting officers sought ASA recruits among college graduates or dropouts; in the 1950s and early 1960s, this was a white demographic.

The U.S. Army Security Agency Training Center and School had been located since 1951 at Fort Devens. (It had originally been sited at Carlisle Barracks in Carlisle, Pa. to which town my academic career would carry me many years later.) Fort Devens sprawled across the towns of Ayer and Shirley in rural Massachusetts about sixty miles northwest of Boston. In 1963, Devens housed a variety of Army units: elements of infantry, armor, mountain troops, engineers, military police. But the ASA contingent was the largest single group. The school prepared troops for assignments in communication analysis, communication security, radio intelligence, Morse and non-Morse intercept, and crypto-equipment maintenance.

I would spend five and a half months at Fort Devens, from early February to mid-July 1963. In that time I completed two training programs. The first, a six-week-long introductory class in basic analysis (which included a daily typing drill), consisted of a lot of puzzles and word games-- some easy, some difficult. It seemed a sustained test of our wit and our patience. Those of us who passed this course--just about everyone did—and, most importantly, those who qualified for the necessary top-secret cryptographic security clearance--a couple of people did not--moved on to an 11-week course in radio-traffic analysis. This was the real thing; this course showed us what we would actually be expected to do in the field.

We would receive transcripts of intercepted Morse transmissions--it amazed us at first to learn that people were still using Morse code. The enemy (unnamed) would try to mask his identity by constantly changing the "external" characteristics of his broadcasting behaviors: the call signs he employed, the times at which he sent his messages, the frequencies on which he set his radio. His behavior would not be random; he would employ a system that he understood but which we did not. We were not cryptographers: our task was not to decipher his messages. These messages were, in any case, probably undecipherable except by computer. Our unseen enemy radio operators normally communicated with each other using the international Morse Q-Code system created in the early 20th century, a standardized collection of three-letter codes all beginning with the letter Q that every Morse code sender understood and which could be employed as both interrogatories or assertions. For example, "QTR" meant either "what is the correct time?" or "the correct time is_____" and "QRL" meant either "are you busy?" or "I am busy" and "QRS" meant either "shall I send more slowly?" or "send more slowly." No one sent Morse code in an actual spoken or written language. The puzzle we had to solve, as radio traffic analysts, was to figure out who was who in the jumble of intercept transcripts and to determine the pattern by which each enemy radio operator was changing his "external" characteristics so that we could establish "continuity" and, eventually, identity.

We would have "continuity" when we could say something like this:

Radio Transmitter "Alpha" will call himself "ABT7" on Monday, Wednesday, and Friday mornings when he will broadcast at 10:30 GMT (Greenwich Mean Time) using frequency 930. He will call himself "XYZ9" on Monday, Wednesday, and Friday afternoons when he will broadcast at 14:30 GMT using frequency 1220. He will call himself "DEF2" on Tuesday, Thursday, and Saturday mornings when he will broadcast at 11:30 GMT using frequency 850. He will call himself "MNO6" on Tuesday, Thursday, Saturday, and Sunday afternoons when he will broadcast at 17:30 GMT using frequency 1445. He will call himself "TCC7" on Sunday mornings when he will broadcast at 08:50 GMT using frequency 1350.

The reality would actually be more complex than this model suggests because a transmitter would use different call signs when sending and receiving, so there would be twice as many call signs as portrayed here. In any case, figuring this out was challenging and interesting. It required a careful, sustained study and reading of the texts which consisted of the Morse intercept-- typed pages provided by the intercept operators known as "Diddie Bops." We--unimaginatively termed "TAs"--operated like a combination police detective and literary critic. We learned how to keep meticulous logs of every message. Who said what to whom? What questions were asked? What questions were answered or not answered? We were looking for mistakes, for slips, for idiosyncratic patterns in the back and forth of the operators' Q-Code chatter. Was a certain radio operator persistently slow in responding to calls? Did another radio operator repeatedly misuse a certain Q-code? Did someone inadvertently use the wrong call sign and then correct himself? Excellent!

By mid-summer 1963 we had completed the course and I had officially achieved my Military Occupation Specialty (MOS) rating: 982.1. We were eager to get going. Our class was small, about 15 guys. We all hoped for an overseas assignment. We couldn't do anything with our miserable Army salaries in the United States: I was making about $85 dollars a month as a Private E-2. And in the States we were still subject to the worst aspects of Army life: the humiliating, demoralizing drudgery of manual labor--like KP--that was routinely imposed on the lower ranks. Once abroad, we knew, this work was usually done by hired local laborers. I hoped to be sent to one of the ASA bases in Europe, Germany preferably. But there were also interesting places in the Far East--Japan or Korea. There was even a new ASA base now in Vietnam, an alluring prospect. We got our orders in June: about half the class, seven of us, would be sent to Vietnam, including me and two people who had been with me since basic training in Fort Dix, Tom McKelvey and Ron Krueger.

Vietnam. This was exciting news. I had turned 18 in March; I was eager to leave Massachusetts; I'd been eager to leave Massachusetts for nine months. Vietnam held no terrors for me or for any of us--although it was sobering to have to endure bubonic plague shots as a medical precaution. We were foolish and ignorant and arrogant and naïve. But no more foolish and ignorant and arrogant and naïve than the men leading our country into the nightmare of a war that would traumatize and polarize us all.

TO VIETNAM

We departed Fort Devens for Vietnam on the morning of Saturday, July 13, 1963. We travelled under the nominal authority of our "senior" member, a guy named Jim Podall, who--because he had been injured playing basketball and had had to take time to recover--had spent a few months more at Devens than the rest of us and had, therefore, been promoted to the rank of Private First Class (E-3) whereas the rest of us were all still just plain privates. But Jim was really one of us. So it meant that we were undertaking this 13,000 mile, three-day junket effectively without supervision. Glorious freedom!

Leaving Ft. Devens for Vietnam, July 1963. (L to R): Bill Cropsey, me, unknown, Henry Venice, Tom McKelvey, Jim Podall.

We took the train (!) from Ayer to Boston and actually passed through Lexington on the way. I wouldn't see the place again for more than two years. At Logan Airport in Boston we board an American Airlines commercial flight to Chicago for the initial leg of our journey. As I'm about to climb the stairs into the plane, I tap my toes twice on the tarmac for luck and tell myself that I'll be back. My first time on a jet airliner--one of the new Boeing 707s just coming into general service. The stewardesses hand out complimentary cigarettes at departure: Kent filters. From Chicago, another American Airlines jet to San Francisco. A long luxurious flight on a half empty plane in gorgeous summer weather. The stewardesses serving free drinks to us because we are in uniform. The pilot calling out wonders to be seen from 30,000 feet from the right and left sides of the aircraft and even encouraging us to visit the cockpit. Ancient, innocent days.

When we arrived in San Francisco on Saturday afternoon, we decided to stay in the city on our own rather than report to the Oakland Army Depot since our flight to the Far East would not leave until Sunday evening. We were reluctant to give up our last moments of liberty. So we rented cheap rooms in a flop house in the Tenderloin District, got out of our uniforms and spent 24 mythical hours goofing around the city, seeing the sights, riding trolley cars, ogling girls, being rebuffed by imperious maître des at fancy bars, and behaving like mischievous children on the eve of a loopy adventure. I had $11 in my pocket.

The next night, July 14, we reported to Travis Air Force Base and flew off in a chartered Pan Am jet to the Far East via the Great Circle Route: Anchorage--Tokyo--Saigon. All the passengers were military, including a good number of Vietnamese officers who were going home after having completed training programs in the United States. By the time we landed in Vietnam, we had crossed the International Date Line and it was Tuesday, July 16. We collected our duffle bags and were subjected to an initial briefing. This included a warning from an excitable major that we must not, under any circumstances, have sex with the natives because the Vietcong had recruited a cadre of fanatical communist prostitutes who had intentionally infected themselves with venereal diseases resistant to all antibiotics for the express purposes of transmitting killer clap to GIs. We were uncertain whether the major actually believed this story about kamikaze whores or whether higher authorities thought this bit of Grand Guignol would help lower the gonorrhea rate among the enlisted ranks. In any case, thus enlightened, we were driven to our new home: Davis Station, 3rd Radio Research Unit, Army Security Agency, Tan Son Nhut Airport, Saigon, Republic of Vietnam.

THE 3RD RRU

Davis Station, the home of the 3rd RRU, exhibited a handsome geometry. A closed square of about 25 single-story barracks: screen walls with dark-brown mahogany slatted sides--to keep out the rain. Tin roofs. Ceiling fans. Each building holding 12 to 14 soldiers. Cots with mosquito netting and individual wooden wall lockers for uniforms and civvies. Not crowded. In the middle of the square, service buildings: latrines, showers (cold water only), mess halls, a laundry. On the periphery an orderly room, armory, movie theatre, a large, white stucco NCO club, motor pool, guard house, barracks for NCOs and officers. All this surrounded, sort of, by barbed wire entanglements and criss-crossed by low, white wooden fences and interlaced by an intricate system of foot-deep drainage ditches, suggesting the ferocity of the monsoon rains, which continued to fall during the rainy season that would not abate for another several months. A comfortable, pleasant place. Meticulous. We were not waste deep in the muck of a rice paddy.

Tom McKelvey (left) and Jim Podall at the gate of Davis Station. In the background, Vietnamese Army barracks. Summer 1963.

The interior of Davis Station. Summer 1963.

After a few days of routine processing, we were put to work in the Holy of Holies, the Operations Building: a large, windowless former warehouse adjacent to the flight-line, a mile or so from our compound. After you entered through the main doors, you had to show your Top-Secret/ Crypto Security Badge to two armed guards who granted entry, one person at a time, through the inner locked doors. You proceeded along a long corridor past individual offices to a 2-story high workroom that extended across the width of the building. The room was nearly filled with a cluster of metal tables around which we all sat facing each other. This is where we worked. No air-conditioning: just table fans set low so as not to blow our logbooks away. We removed our fatigue blouses and worked in our tee shirts.

The dominating feature of this room was an enormous map--probably 30-feet square--covering the full two floors of the facing wall as you entered the room. And there on the map was a detailed, unit-by-unit presentation of the entire Order of Battle of the Vietcong showing the name and location of every regiment and battalion of the VC. The formal title of this dramatic panorama was COSVN, Central Office of South Vietnam, the U.S. term for what we imagined to be the North Vietnamese political and military command authority in South Vietnam. It was a conception that accorded with our understanding that the war represented an *invasion* of South Vietnam by North Vietnam.

Every day the team of traffic analysts--including me--would receive reams of typescript of Morse intercept the Diddie-Bops had produced over the previous 24 hours and had transcribed into intelligible text. We would log the intercepted messages, confirm the established radio continuity recorded there or try to figure out anomalies or confusions, and hand our results to the Radio Direction Finding (RDF) guys whose job it was to use our information to physically locate the transmitters we were tracking. Our RDF guys were actually Aerial Radio Direction Finding

(ARDF) guys who operated two small single-engine, propeller-driven aircraft--deHavilland L-20 "Beavers"--our "Teenie-Weenie Air Force," as it was called. These planes would go up every day to "shoot" some of the stations we monitored. They'd cruise around going 160 mph at about 3,000 feet--just above the range of machine guns--and the radio technician, huddled behind the pilot, would tune in his ARDF machine at the time and frequency indicated by the traffic analyst and he'd search for the promised call sign. Once he had it, the machine would establish a vector--or azimuth--between the airplane and the transmitter on the ground. The radio tech and the pilot, in conversation over their mics, would move the plane together and try to establish at least three directional vectors from the plane to the transmitter. The goal was to triangulate the vectors, and when they got them to cross--Bingo!--that was where the transmitter was located.

I went along on a couple of these flights, sitting in the co-pilot's seat, as an observer; I could only watch because I couldn't decipher Morse code myself. It was an intense experience to see this plane and its crew zero in on the abstraction that I was calling in my logbook "VHMB 84101" but that was, in reality, according to our military intelligence people, the headquarters radio transmitter of the Vietcong 267th Rifle Regiment and to watch them confirm within about a 400 meter-range the location of this transmitter in a stand of trees in Tay Ninh province northwest of Saigon. The ARDF had been introduced in 1962 to replace the less reliable and more dangerous--to its users--land-based RDF that the 3rd RRU had used when it was first deployed to Vietnam in 1961. In December 1961, a member of the 3rd RRU, James Davis, had been killed in a Vietcong ambush outside Saigon, one of the earliest American casualties of the war, while setting up a land-based RDF site. Our compound would be named after Davis.

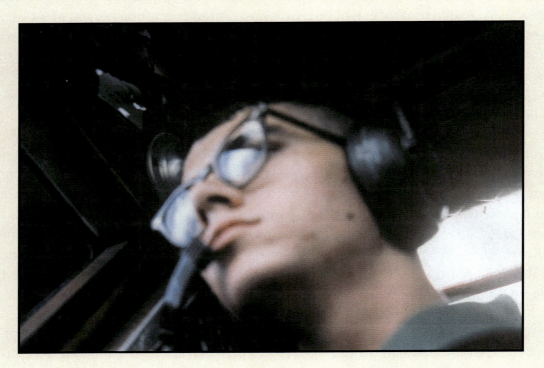

A selfie taken during a flight in a deHavilland Beaver as an observer while one of my networks was being "shot." Fall 1963.

The 3rd RRU was the first American Army unit sent to Vietnam as an intact, coherent organization. It arrived early, in April 1961, and immediately began producing accurate and precise signal intelligence. The Vietcong could not hide. We could tell the Army of Vietnam (ARVN) exactly where the VC were located. Because the U.S. Army had no combat troops in Vietnam, it fell to ARVN to engage the Vietcong and destroy them. But this was not what the government of Vietnam wanted its army to do. Because ARVN was one of the principal pillars of the regime of Ngo Dinh Diem, the government did not wish the army to incur casualties. So ARVN preferred to keep its distance from the Vietcong and avoid close combat. It preferred instead to employ long-range artillery and airstrikes, tactics which did little harm to the VC but which killed lots of old men and women and children and water buffalo and which alienated the rural peasantry from Saigon. This murderous behavior drove the rural population into the arms of the Vietcong who plausibly emerged as the protectors and liberators of the countryside. All our technology and cleverness were for naught. We were on the losing side.

We TAs worked hard in the Ops Building at what we did and took pride in our competence. We believed in what we were doing. I think all of us in those days accepted the conventional wisdom of the Domino Theory--that we had to stop the spread of international communism, that we should defend "democratic" South Vietnam from the "foreign" communist northern invader. I accepted that conventional wisdom. Guys would work overtime and come in on their days off, in civilian clothes, to make sure their portfolios were accurate and up-to-date. There was a strong sense of teamwork and shared values among the enlisted ranks and our operations officers and non-commissioned officers. But we had no patience with military formalities and routines: our uniforms were sometimes unkempt and our hair was sometimes too long. After the Beatles made their first startling appearance in early 1964, the warrant officer who worked in our shop would refer to me affectionately as "my Beatle" because he thought I always needed a haircut.

The Ops gang gathered in the "Papillon" Bar in Saigon, Spring 1964. A mix of TAs, Diddie Bops, linguists--enlisted men, non-commissioned officers and officers. I'm second from the top of the stairs, far right.

Persistent, nagging conflict arose between our operations leaders and our company leaders. Our operations officers and non-commissioned officers, on the one hand, tolerated (and perhaps even relished) our bohemian ways because we produced reliable signals intelligence. They knew our work was good. Our company officers and non-commissioned officers, on the other hand, cared only about the sharpness of the creases in our uniform trousers and the shine of our combat boots. Those were their measures of our values as soldiers. The 3rd RRU had been the first Army unit in Vietnam awarded the Meritorious Unit Commendation. Our company commander concluded that since the citation had been awarded in early 1963, when the unit was populated with notoriously slovenly ranks, he could get us a second award if he shaped us all up and made us dress correctly and polish our belt buckles. He was a shithead, in other words. He was assisted in his mischief by the company first sergeant, a humorless martinet with a shock of white hair whom we referred to as "White Snake." Under the direction of these two clowns, we were constantly subjected to harassing barracks inspections and assorted distracting personal affronts the Army specializes in designing under the general rubric of "chickenshit."

Actually, for the most part, life at Davis Station was not unpleasant. The barracks were comfortable. The food was not bad. You got used to the cold showers. The NCO club offered decent hamburgers, plenty of beer, potent mixed drinks for 25 cents, and dreadful live Vietnamese rock bands. We were a literary bunch, and we spent a lot of time lounging around on our bunks in our underwear reading books: John O'Hara, "Appointment in Samara;" Theodore White, "The Making of the President 1960;" Peter Ustinov, "The Loser;" Barbara Tuchman, "The Guns of August;" James Baldwin, "Giovanni's Room;" James Jones, "From Here to Eternity." There were no television stations in Vietnam then, but we had free movies in our own theatre every night. There were a couple of guys who knew how to run a 35 mm projector, and most of the time they managed to get the reels loaded in the correct order, and if they didn't, we'd rant and stamp our feet, and after 10 minutes or so, they would usually stop the machine and put on the right reel. I remember seeing "Gypsy" and "West Side Story" and "Barabas" and "Dr. No" (the first James Bond film, a hoot!) and "To Kill a Mockingbird" and "Donovan's Reef," and probably 25 other movies that year in Vietnam.

CRISIS

By the time we got to Vietnam in the summer of 1963 the Diem regime was in turmoil. A "Buddhist Crisis" had erupted between the Catholic Diem and Buddhist leaders in a country that was 70 percent Buddhist. In May, government troops had fired on Buddhist demonstrators in Hue; in June, a Buddhist monk had burned himself to death at a busy intersection in downtown Saigon to protest government crackdown on the pagodas. Photographs of the self-immolation were on front pages around the world. In August, Diem declared martial law and his troops raided pagodas and arrested hundreds of monks. Diem and his family--including especially the despised sister-in-law, Madame Nhu--found themselves toxic and isolated. The loyalty of ARVN started to crumble. People began to say openly that things couldn't go on like this. Even the bar girls in downtown Saigon were telling us--discreetly--that things were coming to a head, and that Madame Nhu needed to go.

As the political order within the country deteriorated, American optimism about the course of the war and its confidence in Diem faded. In March 1963, the American commander in Vietnam, the spectacularly incompetent General Paul Harkins, had boasted that "the military phase of the war can virtually be won in 1963." In May, Secretary of Defense Robert McNamara was reporting that he was "tremendously encouraged" by the military progress of the war. McNamara and General Maxwell Taylor, Chairman of the Joint Chiefs of Staff, returning from a visit to South Vietnam in October, told President Kennedy that "the military campaign has made great progress and continues to progress." In fact, by September 1963, the U.S. Ambassador, Henry Cabot Lodge, reported to Washington that the situation in Vietnam was "worsening rapidly...the time has arrived to use what effective sanctions [we have] to bring about the fall of the existing government and the installation of another."

These undercurrents percolated all summer and fall. Meanwhile we explored Saigon.

SAIGON

The city was seductive. A gracious, French colonial place with broad, tree-lined boulevards, handsome squares and landscaped parks. At its center, the red brick nouveau gothic Cathedral of Notre Dame facing across the street the white metal-clad Belle Epoque central post office often erroneously attributed to Gustave Eifel. The downtown buildings were distinctly Gallic: three- or four-story concoctions in soft lavender stucco with pale fillagrees and wrought iron balconies. The taxis were all diminutive blue and yellow Renaults. Some shop-keepers along the main street, Tu-Do, still called it Rue Catinat. The open terrace of the Hotel Continental spilled from the dark interior of its splendid copper bar, past enormous porcelain terrenes from which there sprouted otherworldly palms, onto the brilliant sunlit square anchored by the baroque Carrera marble opera house.

It was always hot in Saigon, even at night. Nothing was air-conditioned then. Large ceiling fans turned lazily in every room, but they made no difference. The air was heavy and lubricious, thick with the smell of flowers and food and people and toilets and sex. The city was busy, but it moved slowly and quietly. A lovely place with lovely people. It was a large city--already 1.5 million inhabitants in 1963--but felt small. Later, with the escalation of the war, a flood tide of refugees would push the population up over 2.2 million by 1972 and ghastly slums would proliferate everywhere, but none of that had happened when I was there. We had free access to Saigon most of the time, and because it was deemed important to minimize the American presence in the country, we were forbidden to wear uniforms in the city. We welcomed the prohibition. I would sometimes go to Saigon alone, wander about for the entire day, shooting slides of this or that, and never encounter either another American or another Caucasian.

Tu-Do Street., downtown Saigon. Fall 1963.

One night, returning late from an evening downtown, I strolled alone into the large mosque on Dong Du Street. I removed my shoes and wandered through the empty white and lime green rooms. The place glowed in the full moon. I sat for a time in a bench in one of the gardens where it was extraordinarily quiet. The only time I'd ever been in a mosque.

My bunkmates in Barracks 22 decided shortly after I arrived--once they discovered that I was still a virgin--that it was incumbent upon them to remedy this unnatural and retarded condition. Ample resources were available in Saigon. A delegation of my colleagues bundled me off to the city under the leadership of an exuberant prankster from New York with the inspired name of Robert Divine who was about to complete his tour of duty in Vietnam. This gang herded me through a couple of bars for preliminary bottles of Biere 33--the potent local brew pronounced "BAH-Mee-Bah--and we then descended on a brothel along the Saigon River where a transaction was quickly arranged and successfully completed.

I was pulling myself unsteadily together and rejoining my buddies in the main room of the thatched hut compound where all this was taking place, when a couple of two-and a-half-ton trucks pulled up outside and a huge commotion of shouting and whistles and the clatter of military impedimenta erupted around the huts. The place was being raided. ARVN had apparently decided that the brothel was a Vietcong sanctuary. The door burst open and a squad of ARVN heroes in battle gear and helmets strode in and braced us against the walls. A Vietnamese soldier, about four feet tall, pushed the muzzle of his M-1 under my chin forcing my head back against a door frame. I found myself staring up through the open roof at a star in the sky and thought: this is the last thing I will ever see because I am going to be shot in the head by a dwarf in a whorehouse.

But Divine was unfazed. He laughed and brushed aside the Vietnamese soldier holding him against a wall--who did not shoot him--and proclaimed that everything was fine, a mere misunderstanding, that we were Americans. No problems, no problems. He announced that we had been sent here personally by Jackie Kennedy to take care of our valiant Vietnamese allies. You gentlemen want some cigarettes? Marlboros? Maybe some beers from the shop next door? BAH-Mee-Bahs? Careful with those rifles, my friends! And then he slapped my assailant on the top of the helmet. Steady there with that dangerous firearm, that's our new guy! Which did not cause this character to shoot me. And, yes, they would like some Marlboro cigarettes. Of course: Marlboros, excellent cigarette; Americans, very, very good. No problems. So, I think we'll just be going along now, my dears. No, no, keep the pack! Thank you, children, we'll show ourselves out. Ta ta, darlings! And none of us was shot.

We behaved like a colonial army lording it over the little yellow people. No, we *were* a colonial army. We treated them with disdain and condescension. We called them "zips." Fraternity boys on a lark. Shameful.

Not everything was shameful, actually.

I met Sara Thu about two months after getting to Vietnam. She worked in the "California Bar" in downtown Saigon as a hostess, a "bargirl" in the current parlance. According to Madame Nhu's strict regulations governing the comportment and dress of female employees of bars, these women could not mingle physically with customers; they had to stay behind the bars and wear modest white tunics and slacks. Sara was an elegant, intelligent Eurasian woman: Vietnamese mother and French father. She spoke, in addition to Vietnamese, Cambodian, French, and passable English. She was 20, two years older than I. And she was beautiful. She liked me and she allowed me to buy her out of her evening hours at the bar so that we could go to movies or to dinner in Cholon, the Chinese section of the city. She was not a prostitute; you could not buy her. It was awhile before we became lovers, but eventually it was clear to people that I was her American friend. She moved to a new bar, the very classy "Le Colisee," which had good food and attractive hostesses. It became our regular spot. I cared deeply for Sara; I think I loved her. But in the end, I would leave Vietnam and we would part, and she would disappear into the vortex of the war.

Sara Thu.

A COUP, AN ASSASSINATION, AND A BOMBING

The domestic political crisis that had been building in Saigon across the summer and fall of 1963 erupted on November 1 when a clique of senior army generals launched a coup to overthrow the Diem regime. It was a Friday, shortly after noon. We were all bending over our message log entries around the cluster of metal tables in the middle of the work room in the Ops Building when one of the officers from our military intelligence desk dashed in, all aflutter, whispered something to our senior non-com, Sergeant First Class Don Cubbison, and dashed back out. "Cubby" was a very cool and terrifying man with a deaths-head stare. "Something's up," he said quietly. "We're closing down." This was ominous. We were returning to the compound.

At Davis Station we assembled in formation on the main company street, and the company commander--the one who wanted us to polish our belt buckles--began to address us, telling us in a rambling monologue that we were receiving confusing and contradictory reports of unusual movements by ARVN units around the capital and that it was unclear what was going on in downtown Saigon. As he was attempting to speak, an astounding display unfolded before our eyes. Over his left shoulder, high in the cloudless blue sky to our right above the airport and in the direction of Saigon, there appeared five T-28 fighter/ground-support aircraft of the Vietnamese air force flying in echelon formation. These ancient, propeller-driven airplanes droned along at an altitude of about 4,000 feet and then, one at a time, each plane peeled away from the formation and turned into a slow, steep dive toward the city and--as the 200 of us watched transfixed-- white smoke suddenly swirled backwards from their wings and, after a few seconds, we heard the rattle of their machine guns from across the miles. They were strafing targets in Saigon. The presidential palace, perhaps! And then each plane would pull up with agonizing slowness from its dive and the next one would follow. Like a scene from "Victory at Sea."

Not knowing what might happen next, fearful that in the chaos, the Vietcong might launch an attack on Tan Son Nhut, we got orders to fortify Davis Station. Foxholes would be dug and sandbags would be filled, and weapons would be issued. There were contingency plans for such an emergency. Unfortunately, no one had told us about them. I learned at this moment that according to the undisclosed plans, I had been assigned to a three-man 50-calibre machine gun crew. I was, in fact, the designated gunner. So the two other guys--whom I hadn't met before-- and I trudged to the armory to collect the machine gun. It was a hideous, gigantic monster that needed to be assembled on a heavy tripod. I was supposed to sit on a metal seat slung from the tripod and hold the dual triggers with both hands while the other two characters fed belts of ammunition into the breech. But I had no idea how to clear the thing or prepare it for firing. Our executive officer, a first lieutenant, came by to inspect us and expressed astonishment at our ineptitude. But in the end he wasn't able to get the thing to work either. We finally lugged the brute out to a perimeter position and pointed it generally toward where we imagined dangerous people might lurk. We tried to assemble it there, but we found that we ended up with parts left over. We determined that if we were attacked by anyone, we would throw these superfluous pieces of metal in the direction of whoever tried to infiltrate our nest.

No one attacked Davis Station that night. But the ARVN generals toppled Diem and they killed him and his brother, Ngo Dinh Nhu. A few days later, when we were able to visit Saigon again, we saw vivid physical evidence of the sharp fighting that had taken place around the presidential palace and some government buildings and police stations. The Vietnamese we knew were elated. Everyone cheered us in the bars and offered us free drinks and kisses. It was like a city liberated: Paris, 1944. Sara Thu and the women and men she worked with in Le Colisee hated Diem and his bullying, corrupt police. They didn't know much about the generals who had replaced Diem and his gang, but they were sure things would improve. They told us they were certain the war would go better. We thought so too. These illusions would persist.

Three weeks after Diem was killed in Saigon, John F. Kennedy was assassinated in Dallas. It was early Saturday morning, November 23, in Saigon. The first garbled reports came in on Armed Forces Radio and said something about the president and governor being wounded, but I was half asleep and scrambling to make formation and I wasn't sure which president or governor they were talking about.

This was an unusual Saturday morning for us. We were up early to test fire, for the first time, a new rifle--the M-14--which the Army was introducing to replace the stalwart M-1, which the Army had been using for a quarter century and which I had used successfully just a year before in Basic Training. This would be our initial chance to handle these things. In fact, the M-14 would turn out to be such a lousy rifle that the Army would stop using it after only a couple of years. But we couldn't know that that morning, and even if we had, it wouldn't have mattered. We were excited by the prospect of a break from office routine. We relished the lark of going off on a shooting party. Boys playing with guns. And so we piled into a convoy of two-and-a-half-ton trucks and drove off for this diversion. The news we'd partly heard and only partly understood about events in way-off Texas or someplace was set aside.

We drove through the northern suburbs of Saigon and into the lush countryside still ripe with the thick foliage from the waning rainy season. We took photographs of the farmers and children who stared glumly or waved at us. We waved back. We took photographs of each other. Guys mugged for the cameras. We were wearing helmets which we normally never did, and so even to each other we actually looked like soldiers. We drove to a shooting range on Bien Hoa airport about 20 miles north of Saigon and we each fired two magazines from our new M-14s into banks of stationary targets at about 50 yards. We made a terrific racket. Then we got into the trucks and headed back to our barracks at Tan Son Nhut.

The ride home was somber and quiet. We began to absorb what we had heard over the radio. Back at Davis Station, our commanding officer addressed us and confirmed the news: the president was dead. Everyone was silent. There were no questions. The CO told us that nothing had changed; our mission remained the same. We suspected that everything had changed.

In February 1964 the Vietcong killed two of our guys. The 3rd RRU had put together a softball team that played teams from other American units at the airport. Following one of its games, our team had lingered to drink beer and watch a second game in the rudimentary bleachers around the softball field. Three innings into the game, an antipersonnel mine exploded under the bleachers instantly killing Art Glover and Don Taylor, two of our intercept operators, and wounding four or five others. I was in Saigon at the time. When I returned to Davis Station later that night, the place was in an uproar. Security was very tight: extra guards were all over the compound. Everyone was up and lots of people were drinking and shouting and some guys were talking stupidly about how we should get our rifles and "shoot up some fucking zips!" We did not do this. Our rifles were locked away in the armory. But I witnessed this inchoate, murderous rage. I felt some of it. It was the kind of inchoate, murderous rage that would cause Americans troops at My Lai four years later to slaughter Vietnamese women and children and babies because they could not find and strike the real objects of their fear and hatred. We did not harm anyone that night. Our rifles were locked away in the armory.

Art Glover and Don Taylor go home. Tan Son Nhut Airport, Saigon. February 1964

The bombing of the softball field led to increased concern that the Vietcong would select other "soft" targets for terrorist attacks. Surely the softest of these potential targets was the school for American dependent children just outside the main gate of the airport. Incredibly, in spring 1964, there still existed in Saigon a community of American families--principally the wives and children of U.S. diplomats, government officials and senior military officers. These kids attended school in a large, K-12 building that was a sitting duck, guarded in only the most casual way by Vietnamese military and civil police. Someone noticed that this was insufficient. Beginning in spring 1964, members of other American units in the area were called upon to provide additional security. Of course, this is not what we were trained to do, but since there were no U.S. military police or combat troops in Vietnam, the job fell to us. So I spent a couple of days nervously patrolling the halls of the school, all dressed up like a real soldier with a helmet and a rifle (unloaded lest there be an accident).

I think those two days may have been the scariest moments I spent in Vietnam. I was a geeky traffic analyst. If a squad of veteran Vietcong rifleman with Kalashnikovs barged into the place, I knew that I and the other 3rd RRU guys would be wiped out. And I knew that we would not be able to protect the kids who would be butchered in the crossfire.

But it didn't happen. The Vietcong did not attack the school. And shortly thereafter, the dependent families were all sent home and the school was shut down.

COMM CHANGE

For the first nine months I was in Vietnam, the Vietcong stations I monitored continued to employ the same external operating procedures--the same call-signs, frequencies, and dialing schedules--that my predecessors had plotted and mapped and handed over to me. The Vietcong had altered virtually nothing in almost two years. I simply confirmed that the puzzle had been correctly solved. Easy. One night in May 1964 this suddenly, dramatically changed. The Vietcong instituted a "Comm Change:" the introduction of a system-wide new pattern of external operating procedures. To us, all became chaos. We didn't know who was who; our Diddie-Bops didn't know to whom they were listening. The reams of intercept delivered to the desks of the TAs were impenetrable. Among the 20 of us in the TA shop, we didn't know which of us should receive which pile of undifferentiated, indecipherable pile of typescript. This was exactly what we were trained to do, but we felt lost. It was as if 10,000 tiny jigsaw puzzle pieces belonging to 200 different puzzles had been suddenly dumped on our desks. We knew, approximately, what the finished puzzles were supposed to look like, but we didn't know, at first, which pieces belonged to which puzzle. We started working 16-hour days, desperate to make sense of the mess.

After five days or so, we began, gradually to re-assemble the outlines of the old networks. The Vietcong radiomen would make mistakes and sometimes use their old call-signs, and this would allow us to glimpse identities between the new system and the old. But it was a slog: we had progressed no more than 25 percent toward re-establishing radio continuity when salvation arrived in the form of a delivery from our Nationalist Chinese friends on Taiwan("ChiNat" as opposed to "ChiCom"--Chinese Communist) who had their own military signal intelligence people monitoring the Vietcong. The ChiNats had noticed the Comm Change, of course. Their radio traffic analysts, who were also Morse intercept operators, had tackled the problem and they had solved it. They sent us their solutions in beautiful handwritten script on elegant parcels of neatly-folded grey rice paper. There we found delicately-drawn, precise diagrams of the military networks we--and they--were tracking with detailed explications of the new and old operating procedures establishing the identity of each station. Radio continuity re-established. Sgt. Cubbison was impressed. "The Chinks are good," he said.

LEAVING VIETNAM

As our one-year tour of duty in Vietnam drew to a close--it actually extended over 11 months and one day--the crew that I had come over with in the summer of 1963 turned our attention to where we would be sent next. With the exception of Henry Venice, who was married and wanted to return to the States to be near his wife, the rest of us hoped for another assignment in the Far East. The most attractive option was the newly-activated ASA site in Thailand, not far from Bangkok, which offered the exotic pleasures and inexpensive living of Saigon without the attendant dangers. There were other appealing postings in Asia--the aforementioned sites in Japan and Korea--and a less attractive one on Okinawa, part of Japan. There was also a hilariously repellant option in the North Pacific, at the very tip of the Aleutian archipelago on the island of Shimya, an impossibly cold and isolated place from which the doings of the Soviet armies in Siberia were monitored. Those of us nearing the end of our Vietnam days were invited to indicate our preferred next assignment. Nearly everyone chose Thailand. I did too, but as my second choice, I indicated my readiness to stay on in Vietnam for an additional year. I was deeply drawn to Saigon; it was a compelling, intoxicating city. I suspected, correctly, that I would never again experience anything remotely like it. But in those days, the ASA didn't want its people to spend a second tour in Vietnam. In 1964 they thought the risk of becoming a casualty should be borne equally among all its members. They'd change their minds on this.

I had become close to three guys in my cohort. Ron Krueger was a boyish, merry character who'd been with me since basic training in Fort Dix. We had volunteered together in Fort Devens to paint cartoonish (and subversive) murals in the day room as a way (only partly successful) of avoiding KP. After a couple of years of lounging around Wake Forest, Ron had dropped out and joined the Army. He was good nocturnal company in Saigon. Jim Podall, a big, raw-boned guy, was--like Krueger--from Pennsylvania. Jim had floated on the periphery of Villanova for a few years though it was never clear to me whether he had actually taken classes there. Jim was a bold spirit, always ready for larks and prowls. Tom McKelvey was the third member of this trio. Tom was the only one of us who had actually completed college: he had graduated from the University of Virginia in the spring of '62 and had then volunteered for a three-year enlistment in the ASA rather than allow himself to be drafted for two years and risk ending up in the miseries of an infantry foxhole. This was the shrewd calculus of the economics major. Tom was a thoughtful and intelligent man who possessed a sly and wicked sense of humor. I had memorable adventures and misadventures in Saigon with these good men. Together we waited out our final weeks in Vietnam until eventually, in May 1964, we received our orders: Krueger--the lucky bastard--was going to Thailand; Podall, McKelvey and I were consigned to Okinawa.

As it turned out, Podall's departure was delayed when his replacement didn't show up on schedule and he was kept at the 3rd RRU for an additional month. But on June 16, 1964, Ron Krueger, Tom McKelvey and I flew out of Tan Son Nhut airport for our new assignments. A big crowd from the Ops building showed up at the terminal to see us off. I include some of the pictures taken that day. We departed in a by-then, seeming old-fashioned, very noisy, propeller-driven DC-6 to Clarke Field in the Philippines where Krueger left us for his flight to Thailand. Tom and I continued on to Kadena Air Base on Okinawa and from there, after a short drive, to Torii Station, site of the 51st United States Army Security Agency Special Operations Command, part of the Joint Sobe Processing Center (JSPC). Our new home.

Ron Krueger, Tom McKelvey, and I leaving Vietnam. Tan Son Nhut Airport, Saigon. June 1964.

The Ops gang gathered at Tan Son Nhut to see us off.

TORII STATION

This new home was a massive place, sprawling over hundreds of acres, in the Yomitan prefecture along the southwest coast of Okinawa--a gently sloping, rocky plateau that eventually slid into the East China Sea at Hagushi Bay. It was precisely here, on April 1, 1945--one week after I was born--that the American 10th Army and the 1st and 6th Marine Divisions had come ashore to begin the invasion of Okinawa, the single bloodiest battle in the Pacific war. Nineteen years later all was quiet. The Yomitan slope was filled now with a large American military post: enormous, gloomy, three-story cinder-block barracks, Quonset huts, motor pools, a big consolidated mess hall, NCO and officers clubs, a library, a movie theater, a bowling alley, an ice cream parlor, guard houses, operations buildings, a laundry, a chapel, extensive antenna fields, a softball field, basketball courts and an entrance gate decorated with two large bright-red interlocking Japanese Shinto shrine gates from which the place derived its name. The distant ocean was startling cerulean blue. But Torii Station itself was drab and utilitarian: all bunker grey-green and cement. Every quotidian feature of American small-town routines compressed into military monoliths without grace or wit. Unrelieved dullness.

A barracks at Torii Station. Okinawa. Summer 1964.

Tom McKelvey and I had been at Torii Station only a few days and were still completing our routine in-processing protocols, when a clerk in the personnel office looked up from our paperwork and brightly informed us that we were about to be promoted. What? We hadn't even reported to duty yet in our new Operations Building! No one knew if we could read or write or speak English. Doesn't matter, said the clerk: special orders from Pacific command. Anyone serves in Vietnam gets promoted.

Tom and I couldn't believe it. This would be our third bump in rank in 11 months. The two of us, who had coincidentally joined the Army on the same day in 1962, had been routinely promoted to Private First Class (E-3) in July 1963 shortly after getting to Vietnam. Seven months later, in February 1964, we had been promoted to Specialist/4 (E-4) for work competently done at the 3rd RRU. We could not reasonably expect another advance in rank for at least a year. To be promoted again, after just four months, to Specialist/5 (E-5) was inconceivable. And E-5 was a big deal! The rank equivalent of a three-stripe sergeant. E-5s and above were not subject to menial labor details. E-5s and above did not have to go through the chow line in the mess hall; they were served their meals by waiters who cleared their tables afterwards. E-5s and above got to drink at the bar in the private lounge in the NCO club. *Spec-fucking-5!*

This sudden, utterly unmerited promotion did not sit well with our new mates. In fact, it provoked considerable anger and resentment of Tom and me, the "Saigon Twins," as we were soon dubbed. It was not only the outrageous unfairness of this unwarranted advance in rank to two entirely untested colleagues. Our promotions triggered a series of practical, logistical consequences in our barracks that pissed off a lot of people. Because of their rank, Spec/5s did not have to sleep in the open bays with the rest of their enlisted colleagues; Spec/5s were entitled to semi-private rooms. So Tom and I promptly took possession of a two-man room vacated by two departing Spec/5s which some of our colleagues--long-serving Spec/4s anticipating soon-to-come promotions and coveting the rooms they hoped to inherit with those promotions--now suddenly saw snatched away by the pretenders from Saigon. Our initial unpopularity was possibly exacerbated by an idiosyncratic feature of our uniforms. As veterans of Vietnam, we wore on the upper right shoulder the bright red and gold unit patch of the Military Assistance Command Vietnam (MACV). Only people who had served in a combat zone displayed insignia on their right shoulders after departing that command. This garish icon invited derision and made Tom and me feel conspicuous and self-conscious.

It helped only a little when Jim Podall showed up from Vietnam a month later. And, of course, he was immediately promoted and, of course, he immediately got someone's semi-private room too. Now the "Saigon Triplets."

BACK TO WORK

The Joint Sobe Processing Center (JSPC) was an inter-service--Army, Navy, Air Force--communications intelligence operation created to monitor the military capabilities of Red China. I was assigned to the desk that oversaw the Shanghai Military District. It was dull work. Strategic stuff, lacking all the tactical urgency that lent significance and immediacy to what we had been doing in Vietnam. We understood that the Chinese were trying to develop a nuclear bomb and we knew that at one level it was important to try to detect evidence of unusual communications traffic among Chinese military units indicating that the testing of this weapon might be imminent. But this seemed abstract. No one was suggesting that the Chinese were going to actually use this bomb or that we were going to actually do anything to prevent them from getting one. And, in fact, they did get one: they detonated their first nuclear device in mid-October 1964. We hardly noticed anything unusual in our communications monitoring prior to the test. Little that we did at JSPC seemed very interesting or very important.

All eyes were on the place we had been, on Vietnam. In the first days of August 1964--just six weeks after McKelvey and I had left Saigon--an American destroyer and three North Vietnamese PT boats engaged in a brief shootout in the Gulf of Tonkin off the coast of North Vietnam. The details of the incident were murky. It is now clear--more than a half-century later--that the Johnson administration misled the public about those details and fabricated a second incident entirely to secure from Congress the passage of a joint declaration, the Gulf of Tonkin Resolution. It empowered Johnson "to take all necessary steps, including the use of armed force, to assist [any threatened Southeast Asian country] requesting assistance in defense of its freedom." This would be the legal basis for the Johnson administration's war against North Vietnam for the next four years.

Johnson's immediate recourse would be the use of air power. He launched a series of sustained air strikes against targets in the North. No U.S. combat troops were committed to Vietnam in 1964. The 23,000 American soldiers in Vietnam that year were technically "advisors," as I and the other members of the 3rd RRU had been.

As McKelvey and I watched these developments in mid-1964, we supported Johnson. We continued to believe in the Domino Theory. We thought South Vietnam was being invaded from the North under the guise of an indigenous guerilla war. We thought that Beijing and ultimately Moscow were behind this invasion. We believed measured, careful escalation--relying upon our demonstrably superior airpower--was a prudent, rational next step. We both, I think, harbored doubts about the wisdom of being drawn into a massive land war in Asia. We had both followed, at a distance, the sober reporting of journalists like Neil Sheehan and David Halberstam whose skeptical, first-hand assessments of the American efforts in Vietnam in 1963-64 had provoked the fury of the Johnson administration. (Halberstam's classic analysis of the origins of the war, "The Making of a Quagmire," would be published in spring 1965.) McKelvey and I were prepared to entertain doubts about the rosiest of predictions that American policy-makers might assert about the future of Vietnam under U.S. tutelage, and we understood that the Vietcong were, in fact, tough, formidable foes. We both knew enough history to recall that a Vietnamese army had humbled and defeated a European army at Dien Bien Phu just 10 years earlier. But we believed--we wanted to believe--it was not Lyndon Johnson's intention to send hundreds of thousands of American soldiers into the rice paddies and mountains of that dangerous place. We did not doubt, however, that the erratic lunatic, Barry Goldwater, would drop hydrogen bombs on the place in the blink of an eye. Which was why, among many reasons, good Connecticut moderate Republican Tom McKelvey voted for Lyndon Baines Johnson for president of the United States in November 1964.

I did not vote in that election; I was still too young.

TV AND BOWLING

Our off-duty lives at Torii Station passed uneventfully, marked by sports and movies and television and reading and lots of drinking.

We played flag football in the fall and softball in the spring; we bowled in winter and played basketball on the outdoor courts in summer. The movie theater had comfortable seats and the films were always run in proper sequence. The movies consisted of regular-feature fare: the inspired Peter Sellers Inspector Clouseau farces--"The Pink Panther" and "A Shot in the Dark"-- and routine Jack Lemmon comedies: "Good Neighbor Sam" and "How to Murder Your Wife." The second James Bond adventure, "From Russia With Love." And there were some great films: the stirring and hilarious "Tom Jones," "Dr. Strangelove" (I had never seen anything like it, nor had the fat, clueless, sergeant's wife in front of me who stood up and said to him as she left, "I don't get it."), "The Manchurian Candidate" (stunning and unsettling) and "A Hard Day's Night" (my first intimation that something very significant was happening on the musical and cultural level back in the States). I continued to read a lot: Arthur C. Clarke, "Childhood's End;" Norman Mailer, "An American Dream;" Will and Ariel Durant, "Caesar and Christ;" Mark Twain, "The Mysterious Stranger." And the beginning of all social and political wisdom, Joseph Heller's "Catch-22." (A friend, one of Torii Station's librarians, reported that he had catalogued it among the non-fiction.)

Almost every night, it seemed, McKelvey and I would wander down from our room for a late beer to the "Annex," a double Quounset hut with a snack bar, board games, slot machines and a television set--the first TV we had seen in nearly a year. We'd eat cheeseburgers, drink Rheingold lagers and watch dumb TV shows--"Combat" with Vic Murrow and "The Fugitive" with David Janssen and the moronic "Beverly Hillbillies." In the autumn of 1964 we got to view the Tokyo Olympics live, in vivid black and white, and in real time, since we shared a common time zone with the Japanese capital. We were, after all, part of Japan.

We rarely left Torii Station to explore the small towns in southern Okinawa. I took a one-week R&R sightseeing vacation to Taipei, Taiwan in February 1965, but I don't recall a single expedition to Naha, the capital of Okinawa. After the delights of Saigon, Okinawa was a not unexpected disappointment.

One of the few trips I took off-post was enlightening in surprising ways. Sometime in the summer of 1965, late in my tour, I accompanied one of my buddies on a drive around the northern part of the island, the areas of Okinawa not infested by U.S. military installations. We cruised along the peripheral highway next to the oceans. The place was beautiful: lush fields, verdant, low mountains and spectacular coral beaches on both the Pacific and East China Sea coasts. Paradisal. My friend was driving a Japanese car he had just purchased: a bright red, two-seat convertible. It was called a Honda. When we returned to Torii Station, everyone gathered in the parking lot to examine this curiosity. We found the little thing cute and amusing. We noted that its drive train--the mechanism that connected the engine to the rear axle--consisted of a heavy chain that extended underneath and outside the car. Someone wondered if our friend intended to bring the car back to the States after his tour of duty ended. Much hilarity. "Made in Japan" in those days meant "cheap," "junk," "worthless," "crap." Japanese industry, having been flattened in World War II, had been able in the ensuing decades to produce little more than children's whistles and kazoos and cap guns and tin ukuleles. And now this funny little convertible with a chain drive train. Maybe good enough for a spin around Okinawa, but cars like this could never make it in New York or California or Tennessee, we all agreed. Cars like this could never compete with a Ford or a Chrysler or an Oldsmobile.

GETTING OUT

Almost as soon as I arrived on Okinawa, I began setting in motion a plan to secure an "early out" from my three-year enlistment. The Army granted soldiers who had been admitted to a college or university up to a three-month early discharge. I wanted to start college in the fall of 1965, two months before my scheduled discharge on Nov. 13, 1965. I needed a formal letter of admission that included the date when I would have to report to campus to register for classes. The Army would release me one week before that date. A straight-forward process. But to which schools should I apply?

Money was still an issue: I could not afford to enroll as a residential student. I was saving a lot of my E-5 pay--about $275 per month--but I would have to live at home and commute to class as before, and therefore my choice of schools was limited to colleges in greater Boston. I was not going to repeat the unhappy experience of the fall of 1962: Boston College was out. I needed a couple of "safe" choices which I thought would assure me of ready acceptance. I settled on Suffolk University--an honest, plebian commuter school in downtown Boston--and Boston University-- the sprawling mega-university with high ambitions for itself along the Boston side of the Charles River. At my mother's urging, I applied to Harvard as well, although I entertained no illusions that Harvard would be impressed by my mediocre high school grades.

My mother also sent me a Tufts catalogue, and I liked what I saw. Tufts was co-ed; the general education program imposed no mathematics on the unwilling; the laboratory science requirement could be satisfied with geology; the foreign language department offered German, my preferred choice. While my family had had long associations with Catholic colleges and universities and Tufts was historically Protestant (and now secular), there was, in fact a family connection with Tufts: one of my mother's cousins--Frankie Reed--had graduated from Tufts in the 1950s, and Dr. Paul Sheeran--our family dentist and Ann's long-time employer and mentor--was a product of Tufts well-regarded dental school. Tufts became my choice. But it was a competitive place, and I was not at all sure I would be admitted.

That I was, in the end, admitted to Tufts was due I think primarily to my mother's tireless advocacy on my behalf. She pestered the admissions office with endless phone calls and appeals and she wore them down. She was a fearsome warrior, and I think they finally capitulated from exhaustion. My inclusion did nothing to enhance the academic profile of their incoming freshman cohort in fall 1965. Maybe they wanted a little diversity, a term not employed in the college admissions business in those days: I would be the only veteran in that group of 500 or so men and women. For whatever reason, Tufts said yes. As did Suffolk and Boston University. Harvard said no.

By mid-summer 1965, everything appeared to be in place. I had my letter of acceptance from Tufts which stated that I needed to appear in person on the Medford campus on Thursday, September 18 to meet my academic advisor and register for classes. I had submitted the paper work for an "early out" which had been approved: I would be discharged from the Army at the Oakland Army Terminal in California no later than Wednesday, September 8; I would leave Okinawa the previous day, Tuesday, September 7. In early July I had my exit interview with my commanding officer, Major William Rigo, whose task it was on these occasions to persuade enlisted men leaving the Army to re-enlist. Rigo was a good man and he knew me: he understood that there was no chance of talking me into signing on for another three-year hitch, but he had to go through the exercise. We sat in his office and drank coffee and engaged in small talk as he looked over my service record. After a few minutes he asked me how old I was. I told him I was 20. He pondered my service record a bit longer and then he looked up at me again. "I think you should go to college," he said quietly. I agreed. "Yes," he said, "I think you should go to college." We shook hands, and we saluted. And I did not re-enlist.

At the last moment, everything threatened to unravel. The war was going very badly in Vietnam. Johnson sent in the first U.S. combat troops in April when he dispatched 3,500 Marines to Da Nang. Their mission was technically defensive: they were to protect the Da Nang airfield from the kind of night attack that had badly damaged the airfield at Pleiku the previous month, but before long the restive Marines were engaged in seek and destroy missions on their own. Army combat units followed in June. Throughout the spring and summer, despite the increased weight of American air support, the course of the ground war followed an unmistakably negative trajectory: the Vietcong--more and more augmented by North Vietnamese units--was winning and the South Vietnamese Army was losing. The new U.S. commander in Vietnam, William Westmoreland, told Johnson he needed American combat troops to win the war. In June, Secretary of Defense McNamara recommended to Johnson that the United States commit 175,000 troops to Vietnam and that the President call up the Army Reserve and National Guard. Without knowing the details of any of this, we understood enough from the top secret communications that crossed our desks that something big was coming in the way of a major announcement regarding Vietnam. We anticipated news of a large troop deployment. We heard rumors of a possible Reserve and National Guard mobilization. And we feared, in that event, that our enlistments would be extended. No "early out" for me. Perhaps no discharge at all for any of us in 1965.

Johnson spoke to the nation on July 28, 1965. We crowded around the TV set in the Annex with our Rheingolds. I was terrified. Johnson did not want to be the first president to lose a war, he would say to his aides. But he also did not want the country to think this was going to be too uncomfortably large a war, one that would ruin his plans for the Great Society. So Westmoreland would get his soldiers, but he would not get them all at once. Gradually. Johnson announced a gradual war. He would increase the number of troops in Vietnam by 50,000. He would increase the draft from 17,000 per month to 35,000. But Johnson would not call up the Reserves and he would not mobilize the National Guard. Not too much inconvenience to civilians. And no mention of extended enlistments. I would get out. More Rheingolds, all around!

I longed desperately to get out of the Army. While I welcomed the camaraderie of the people I served with--indeed, my friendship with Tom McKelvey would endure for the rest of my life--I was appalled by the Army as an institution. My romantic notions of military life had been thoroughly exorcised. I loathed the Army's innate conservatism and lack of imagination, its suspicion of anyone different or unusual or clever. I loathed its hostility to wit or irony, its humorless self-importance and pomposity, its willful small-mindedness and coarseness. I loathed it because it insisted on conformity and despised the individual. I vowed that if, in later years, I were to look back with fondness on moments that occurred during my time as a soldier--if I came, on one level, to treasure that extraordinary adventure that was my year in Vietnam--I would not permit that nostalgia to cause me to forget the stifling, soul-deadening everyday reality of life in the United States Army.

A typhoon slammed into Okinawa during my last month of work in August 1965, and under days of torrential rain, we pulled some 12-hour shifts in the Operations Building. In one of those long sessions, I composed for myself a summary analysis of my thoughts on the Vietnam War. Fifteen handwritten pages of tendentious, sophomoric prose. My best Trevor-Roper. I attempted to cast the war in grand geopolitical terms using the biggest dominoes. The war was, of course, I asserted, an invasion: "to deny that North Vietnam [I wrote] with the overt support of Communist China has directed and supported the Vietcong offensive in South Vietnam is to indulge in the most dangerous form of self-deceit." We had to successfully defeat this invasion in order to teach the Chinese a lesson. "The Chinese Communists must be made to realize that their territorial and economic aims [I concluded] cannot be achieved through force of arms...because no nation has the right to enforce its will upon another." The argument was smug and conventional. Up to a point, it was unobjectionable. But it was ignorant. The Vietnam War--I understand now--was the final stage of the national unification of the Vietnamese people and their liberation from colonial occupation. I didn't know that when I wrote that paper. I would come to understand it in the next few years.

I concluded my work in the Joint Sobe Processing Center in the last days of August 1965 and then I underwent a lengthy security de-briefing. I pledged, under threat of criminal penalty, for the next 30 years to reveal nothing about what I had done or witnessed in the Army Security Agency. At the conclusion of the briefing, I surrendered my Top Secret/Crypto Security Badge. No more secrets.

As I was wrapping up my final, routine out-processing in the Personnel Office a day or two before I left Okinawa, the personnel clerk reached into a large file cabinet next to his desk and handed me a Good Conduct Medal. "Here you go, Specialist MacDonald," he said cheerfully. "Everyone gets one." Actually, everyone does not. Forty-one years later, in 2006, looking through a copy of my service record which I had obtained from the National Personnel Records Center in St. Louis, I noticed that the Good Conduct Medal was not listed among my authorized decorations. Trying to figure out why, I studied my record carefully and noticed under "Specialized Training" the cryptic entry "CrA NonJudPun" dated "24Sep63." What was this? I finally puzzled it out. Way back in September 1963, shortly after arriving in Vietnam, I recall being reprimanded for having one night failed to sign back into the company after returning from Saigon. And for this oversight, the first sergeant--that miserable bastard, "White Snake"--had apparently entered "Non Judicial Punishment" into my permanent service record. This translated to "Bad Conduct." And thus, "No Good Conduct Medal." But the Army had just given me the medal--or at least the clerk in the Personnel Office on Okinawa had given me the medal. I would keep it.

I left Okinawa at 8:15 am, Tuesday morning, Sept. 7, 1965. (One would have thought that it might have occurred to this student of World War II that I was departing Japan precisely 20 years and five days after Japan had surrendered in 1945 thereby ending the Second World War. But that did not occur to me.) McKelvey and Podall and a few other guys accompanied me to the airport to see me off. This was how you did it. I flew out of Kadena Air Base on a chartered Trans Caribbean 707; all the passengers were military personnel or dependents. We flew to Honolulu, re-fueled, then continued on to Travis Air Force Base in California. Having crossed the International Date Line during this 15-hour flight, we arrived in California 15 minutes earlier, local time, on the same calendar day we had left Okinawa.

A bus carried those of us in the Army to the Oakland Army Terminal and we commenced the clamorous process of getting discharged, which like all Army enterprises lurches alternately between outbursts of frenetic pandemonium and freezes of silent paralysis. Time passed. Eventually we managed to shed most of our unwanted gear and unneeded uniforms; eventually most of our paper work was stamped and poked and shuffled and signed and stapled. An indolent captain suggested that as the hour was getting late, perhaps we might finish things up the following day, but we howled in protest and frightened him into a flurry of unaccustomed competence, and he managed to get us paid. I was cashing in weeks of unused leave time, and I was being compensated for long travel back to my place of enlistment. I took my last Army pay--$957 in cash: nineteen $50 bills, one $5 and two $1s. There was an airlines counter as we left the Army Terminal selling discounted tickets. I bought a one-way American Airlines flight to Boston for that evening.

A couple of the guys who'd just gotten discharged with me urged me to join them for a drink in San Francisco where they wanted to visit the topless joints that had recently opened up. Carol Doda at the Condor Club in North Beach was all the rage. I understood at once how quickly what remained of my $957 would disappear in North Beach and declined their invitation. They departed for their adventures in a cab, and I took a separate taxi to the San Francisco airport where I called home--at first I couldn't remember the number--and spoke to my mother to tell her that I would be at Logan Airport the following afternoon. We hadn't heard each other's voices in 26 months.

I drank a beer at the airport lounge. I was, suddenly, all by myself. Exquisite. I told the bartender that I had just gotten out of the Army and was going home to college. He bought me a round.

Red eye from San Francisco. I'd been up for three days straight. Shaving on the plane. Chicago. Reading a novel I could not follow. Boston. Tapping my foot twice at the bottom of the unloading ramp as I had done in July 1963 going the other way. Now my mother rushing me at the terminal doors, trying to take a photo. No photo. Mary and Patty, all grown up. Impressive. Black Mercedes. Nice. Storrow Drive, Route 2, Mass. Ave., Captain Parker. The house with the sweeping porch. Uniform off. Civilian clothes. Home.

Click.